D0915010

PHILOSOPHY—THEOSOPHY—PARAPSYCHOLOGY

PHILOSOPHY
THEOSOPHY
PARAPSYCHOLOGY

Some Essays on Diverse Subjects

by

J. J. POORTMAN, Ph. D.

Professor of Metaphysics in the Spirit
of Theosophy
in the University of Leyden

A. W. SYTHOFF - LEYDEN
1965

LIBRARY OF CONGRESS CATALOG CARD NUMBER: 64-8472

Printed in the Netherlands by A. W. Sythoff, Printing Division, Leyden

PREFACE

I want to thank here as well those who at various times and in various places have translated the following papers from the Dutch as those who have helped me to translate them, viz. Mr. James Brotherhood, Mrs. A. D. Cambier van Nooten, née Bondam, Mr. Robert Lee Wolff and Mr. Trevor S. Preston.

J. J. Poortman

CONTENTS

I

IMMANUEL KANT AND PARAPSYCHOLOGY[1]

It is a familiar aspect of contemporary philosophy that interest in IMMANUEL KANT and his philosophy has greatly declined. This is particularly evident from the small number of philosophers who still call themselves Kantians pure and simple. Incidentally, it might be that this lack of interest in Kant comes more from the fact that the problems posed by him have remained unsolved—by Kant too—than that these problems have no point.[2] In any case Kant remains one of the most important figures in human thought, if only for the multitude of problems which he posed, and for their profundity.

One of the sciences which has come into existence in the last eighty years is that of *parapsychology*. Not that it has already won an undisputed place for itself. The subjects of its research are too strange, too unusual, for that, and above all, if the factualness of the phenomena which it studies is proved, results of this nature form such a threat to various fundamentals of the view of the world now fairly generally accepted,[3] that the hesitancy of many about this branch and task of human knowledge is quite understandable. Nevertheless, as I have heard one of the professors of Leyden University say, anybody who asserts that parapsychology has so far achieved absolutely nothing, has gained no results of any kind, simply demonstrates that he has not acquainted himself with the results of parapsychological research.

Thus on the one hand we have the philosopher Kant, a figure of the eighteenth century with a certain lasting importance, and on the other hand a new science, whose endeavours are perhaps promising, but are in any case stimulating.

We will now briefly investigate the relationship between these two, the connection between Immanuel Kant and parapsychology.

At first sight this appears to be an anachronism. Kant died in 1804. Whilst the name of parapsychology dates from 1889 and only came so strongly to the fore in the last few decades, the scientific study of so-called occult phenomena, which at first was called psychical research, goes back to the foundation of the British Society for Psychical Research in 1882. The better part of a century thus lies between the two. What, then, could Kant have had to do with parapsychology?

Anyone who asks this is too hasty in his judgment. The group of phenomena in which parapsychologists are interested also occurred in much earlier times and attracted attention even then.[4] Those who in former days already adopted towards these phenomena an attitude which was neither credulous nor superstitious, but critical, together with a tendency to investigate them further, may be said to that extent to have practised parapsychology. And although at that time this research was not of a very extensive nature, it becomes especially interesting when they already absorbed themselves in the theoretical consequences thereof.

Now this is precisely what Kant did. The cause was another Immanuel, viz. his older contemporary EMANUEL SWEDENBORG (1688-1772). In Kant's case it first assumed the form of the desire to establish the accuracy of a number of concrete facts said to have occurred as a result of Swedenborg's supposed occult gifts. Kant tells of this in his well-known letter to Charlotte von Knobloch. Three cases were concerned. Swedenborg was alleged to have communicated to the Swedish Queen Luise, the sister of Frederick the Great, something concerning her late brother,[5] about which the Queen was surprised and horrified, since according to her nobody could possibly know anything about this but her brother and herself. Swedenborg was also said to have helped the widow of the Dutch ambassador in Stockholm to find a lost receipt which she needed. Thirdly, there is the story of the fire at Stockholm in 1759, which Swedenborg was supposed to have observed after landing at Göteborg upon his return from England, and thus at a considerable distance from Stockholm, and which he is said to have reported to others before a messenger from Stockholm arrived at Göteborg with the news. In his letter Kant attaches most credence to the last case. According to him, there was no doubt about its correctness.[6]

It will be seen that these three cases display a pattern which also tends to arouse the interest of parapsychologists elsewhere, whilst Kant tried through correspondents to acquaint himself as closely as possible with the facts and, as he states, also approached Swedenborg himself in a letter. All of this may safely be described as a sample of sincere and sound parapsychological activity.

Now Kant returned to these three cases and to Swedenborg in his celebrated essay published in 1766, *Träume eines Geistersehers*.[7] But the tone of this work is quite different. Without its being evident that he was in possession of later information, Kant now doubted the value of these three cases. He now called Swedenborg an arch-fantast. Kant also indulged in theoretical observations on the possibility of entering into contact with the spirit world; these observations do not form the least interesting part of his essay, and we shall come back to them shortly.

Many have been struck by the discrepancy between the attitude which Kant adopted towards Swedenborg in the letter and that in *Träume eines Geistersehers*. Added to this was the fact that there was some uncertainty about the dating of the letter to Charlotte von Knobloch. Now Swedenborg's adherents have tried to prove that the letter was of later date than the essay, so that in the letter Kant revised his unfavourable opinion of Swedenborg expressed in the *Träume*. In our opinion Ernst Benz, the church historian from Marburg, settled the controversy in his *Swedenborg in Deutschland*[8] by demonstrating by means of a passage in a letter from Kant to Moses Mendelssohn that the letter must date from 1763, i.e. from before the *Träume*. It follows that Kant revised his opinion.

But Kant's final judgment on Swedenborg has not yet been established. For in 1821 Pölitz, on the basis of lecture notes, published *Vorlesungen* by Kant *über die Metaphysik*. This publication was rather neglected, until Carl du Prel had part of it reprinted in 1889 under the title *Kant's Vorlesungen über Psychologie*.[8a] Now the importance of these publications is that in them Kant calls Swedenborg's ideas about the spirit world sublime: *sehr erhaben*,[9] whilst there are indications that the notes in question were taken at later lectures, that is to say in Kant's critical period and in a period after the writing of the *Träume*. In other words, Kant also held Swedenborg in esteem in his later life. The well-known historian of philosophy, Max Heinze, subjected the problem of the authenticity and the dating of these notes to a critical examination in a lengthy article in 1894.[10] This examination is in the familiar heavy philological style, with references to mss. L1 and L2, K1 and K2, H, etc. He comes to the general conclusion that Kant's lectures reproduced in the *Vorlesungen* are of earlier date, although the possibility remains open—a possibility which du Prel considers reality—that they also contain later opinions held by Kant, including opinions on Swedenborg.

We shall probably never know the true facts of the case, nor do we need to go further into the matter. For there is no doubt that Kant's comprehensive unfavourable opinion of Swedenborg in the *Träume* greatly determined Kant's attitude, and that this opinion was in close agreement with his later and final philosophical standpoint. To this extent our conclusion with respect to Kant's attitude to parapsychology must inevitably be that it was highly negative. Either he had not succeeded in going into parapsychological facts or he no longer considered himself called upon to do so. He turned against Swedenborg and against the possibility of seership on theoretical grounds. It has been remarked on more than one occasion that Kant does not exactly appear in a good light in this matter. The tone which he uses to discuss Swedenborg in the *Träume* is very unpleasant.[11] It is as if he is shocked at the consequences of his initially fairly favourable opinion of the Swedish scholar in the letter. However this may be, his theoretical attitude with regard to the problems of possible contact with the spirit world is nothing if not consistent and in accordance with the main features of his philosophy.

Now it is all the more remarkable that Kant nevertheless proves not to be too far removed from Swedenborg in various places, including the *Träume*, and precisely in his theoretical observations. In the first place, as has been repeatedly remarked, he states Swedenborg's point of view very well in the *Träume*, even there. He realized the other point of view and its implications well enough.

Now what is at issue in these two points of view? Kant's negative attitude is the product of his conviction that the possiblity of knowing and proving is confined to experience, ordinary experience, and cannot transcend phenomena. In his opinion metaphysics, a knowing of the noumena, or things in themselves, is impossible. At most Practical Reason, with its postulates, can get a little further here. All of this was precisely formulated by Kant in his later or critical period, but in his *Träume* too it already forms the basis of his expositions. He concludes the first, the speculative, part of the *Träume* by saying that phenomena are all that we are permitted to know; on the other hand, positive thought on the life principle, the *geistige Natur*, is impossible, since in the whole of our perceptions no data on it are encountered; the extensive subject of the existence of spirits is therefore something which he can put aside as over and done with; it does not concern him further.[12] Ernst Benz is even of the opinion that it was in particular here, in his controversy with Swedenborg, that Kant became aware of his later critical, anti-metaphysical point of view.[13] However this may be, in any case his rejection of the possibility of knowing the other world, that of spirits, already finds very clear expression in the *Träume*.

To this extent Kant and Swedenborg are doubtless antipodes; while Kant denies the possiblity of contact with that other world, Swedenborg asserts that this contact is a very usual thing for him! For Swedenborg does not belong to the category of seers who go into a kind of trance or state of ecstasy and, having come round again, tell of their experiences; no, according to what he says, the transition from one world or way of perceiving to another is easy and quick for him.[14] Now this does not fit in at all with Kant's philosophy, and it is not so very surprising that Kant tried to dispose of Swedenborg rather roughly.

And yet we cannot get away from the fact that Kant suddenly proves even in the *Träume* not to be too far removed from Swedenborg. This too has its foundation in Kant's doctrine, but in another part of it. There are various themes, such as the existence of God, of the "intelligible" freedom of man and his immortality, which according to Kant can never be known in the ordinary way, and to which he tries to give validity in a roundabout way, viz. by means of the *Postulate der praktischen Vernunft*. It has been said that by so doing Kant let in again at the back door what he had just shown out through the front door (and shown out in his capacity of *Alleszermalmer*, the destroyer of everything, as he has sometimes been described). This is what the late Professor Leo Polak used to call the (according to him false) *pathos* of *praktische Vernunft* or Practical Reason as opposed to the *bathos*, the depth, of *reine Vernunft* or Pure Reason. Now since Kant taught both *reine* and *praktische Vernunft* and what ensues from them, these two worlds must nevertheless have a point of contact even for him somewhere, and according to Kant this point is to be found in individual man. He therefore says in the *Träume*: "Es ist. . . zwar einerlei Subjekt, was der sichtbaren und unsichtbaren Welt zugleich als ein Glied angehört, aber nicht ebendieselbe Person. . .".[15] In other words, the person or we in our ordinary daily consciousness, knowing nothing of that other world, must be distinguished from the individual subject, who is a citizen of both worlds. A further idea which links up with this is that these human subjects among themselves, i.e. in that other world, still firstly belong to the same level or zone and secondly must probably have a more or less activated mutual relationship in that other world. Kant also explicitly states the latter idea; later he even uses for it the expression: the *corpus mysticum der vernünftigen Wesen*, the mystical body of rational beings.[16] But when Kant writes accordingly in the *Träume* about *die unmittelbare Gemeinschaft der Geister*, the immediate community of spirits, and about a *geistige Republik*, a spiritual republic,[17] this is entirely in keeping with Swedenborg's assertion that such a community of spirits existed, and even that he was well acquainted with it. It is here that Kant shows how well he understood Swedenborg. However, he does not do this so that he can entirely reject the ideas thereafter; no, he returns to this theme in the *Kritik der reinen Vernunft*, i.e. in the middle of his critical period, and it is there that he uses this expression *corpus mysticum*.[18] This is consistent and to be expected, too, for besides the critical rejection of knowledge in the ordinary way of matters of the other world, he always adhered to the idea of being aware of that intelligible world by a roundabout way. Both worlds therefore play a lasting role in Kant's philosophy. Various scholars have also been struck by the fact that Kant and Swedenborg used the same terms for these worlds, viz. *mundus sensibilis* and *mundus intelligibilis.* But the great difference is that according to Swedenborg contact and the transition between the two worlds are easy, at least for him, whereas according to Kant there is an enormous chasm between the two. Nevertheless, Kant also accepts this mundus intelligibilis (though in that roundabout way) and to this extent his views are more or less related to Swedenborg's.

These points of contact between Kant and Swedenborg have not escaped the attention of the historians. The well-known commentator of Kant's *Kritik der reinen Vernunft*, Hans Vaihinger, points out that what he calls Swedenborg's influence on Kant cannot be denied, and that it can be indicated in various of Kant's works, including the reference just cited to the *corpus mysticum* in the *Kritik der reinen Vernunft.*[19]

A remark about Carl du Prel (1839-1899) must be inserted here. This isolated thinker boldly advocated a philosophical interpretation of occult phenomena at a time when psychical research or parapsychology had hardly been heard of in Germany. In the Netherlands he inspired Dr. K. H. E. de Jong. Du Prel, however, was unfortunate in his terminology. For instance, he used to call what was later to be christened parapsychology *Mystik*,[20] whilst as a rule this term is employed differently. He called the subject who is aware of that other world *das transzendentale Subjekt.* But it is obvious that Kantianism has something quite different in mind with the transcendental subject, which is all the more cogent when one is inclined (as we are) to restrict the functions of the latter to the One Suprasubject; however, for Du Prel there were many *transzendentale Subjekte.* As stated above, Du Prel republished Kant's *Vorlesungen über Psychologie* in 1889. He was of the opinion that in these lectures an entirely different Kant came to the fore, also in his critical and postcritical period, than the Kant of the *Träume.* Du Prel hoped to find support here for what might be called his own philosophical-parapsychological point of view. But, as already remarked, the dating of these lectures by Kant is not entirely settled. Vaihinger is therefore of the opinion that Du Prel greatly exaggerated in his interpretation of Kant but, he goes on, nor may one fall into the opposite error of entirely denying Kant's positive relationship to Swedenborg.[21]

One might also put it in a different way, and say that an *ambivalence* may be noted in Kant: on the one hand, in agreement with Swedenborg, he continues to accept the existence of another world to some extent, and on the other hand he firmly rejects the possibility of contact with this world, of knowing it. The latter is his official philosophical point of view, which will be shared all the more readily if one rejects the postulates of *praktische Vernunft*. It is this later official point of view that is already strongly apparent in the *Träume*, where it condemns Swedenborg. Benz points out that this opinion of Kant's decided Swedenborg's fate.[22] It became the majority opinion of him. But in itself Kant's argument here is not very strong. For it might be that our experience and the phenomena appearing to us are susceptible to extension. In other respects, too, e.g. vis-à-vis geometry, Kant drew too narrow a line. For instance, other senses may be latent in man. This restriction by Kant of knowledge to ordinary experience gives a rather one-sided impression. This is something which cannot be said beforehand; the facts will have to show who is right. Who knows, perhaps phenomena occur which at first sight seem very unusual; who knows, normal and ordinary contact with another world in a somewhat broader sense may be possible.[23] Du Prel pointed to this possibility in a theoretical respect—and in not too happy a manner—and it has been left to the science of psychical research or parapsychology to take the first practical steps towards experimental proofs of this.

This peculiar attitude on the part of Kant will have to be viewed in a wider context and in its historical perspective. He is by no means the only figure from the seventeenth and eighteenth centuries to display such an ambivalence, such hesitation between two mental attitudes. In many thinkers and scholars in the Modern Age we encounter a mixture of old and new, of traditional and modern views. Kepler concerned himself not only with astronomy, but also with astrology. Hugo Grotius wrote not just legal but also theological works, in which on occasion he demonstrated his sympathy with teachings of the Fathers of the Church.[24] The great Newton also had his mystical side; he made a study of Jacob Boehme. Balthasar Bekker combated many kinds of superstition, but whilst he denied on philosophical grounds the possibility of intervention by the devil, he did not deny the latter's existence. The conviction that there is another world besides the ordinary one which we know was still quite generally held in these centuries. Now Kant's postulates of practical reason (on immortality, intelligible freedom, etc.) may be interpreted as satisfying his need also to find a basis for the traditional belief in a *Jenseits*, a hereafter, a life after death. Since Kant believed that he could not altogether dispense with this, he was after all in a certain respect, however it might be, not so far removed from Swedenborg and the latter's proclamation of the existence of another world and of the possibility of contact with that world.

But—and here lies precisely Kant's ambivalence—his philosophical reflections compel him sharply to reject the possibility of that contact. Here, and also for instance in the rejection of the traditional proofs of God's existence, he is the *Alleszermalmer*. He wishes to base the existence of God, just as much as the existence of an hereafter, solely on a postulate of Practical Reason. He thus accepts both of them, old and new, side by side, so that opposing tendencies of the day clash within him, without his achieving an organic synthesis of them. Nevertheless, it is clear that Kant's scepticism—which is the stronger of the two in him—is rooted in the spirit of his day, viz. in the more modern tendency thereof. This trend of the Modern Age may be called a *positivistic* one, one which wants to confine itself to the obvious, the positive aspects of ordinary experience. It is rather superfluous to point out what enormously important consequences this self-restriction has evinced. The great expansion of natural science, from which we benefit daily in the form of technology, is one of the results of this restriction to the facts of ordinary experience and to the careful study of these facts. But this development was not free from one-sidedness. This showed itself particularly in philosophical thought. Generally speaking, materialism is a form of positivism, viz. that form which prefers to adhere to (ordinary) matter as being the most obvious. It was in these seventeenth and eighteenth centuries that materialism made its appearance in Europe, though it was then confined to a handful of individual thinkers. This was followed in the nineteenth century by a second wave of materialism which—characteristically enough, at the same time as the great expansion of natural science and of its applications—spread and was adhered to in wider circles as well. Immanuel Kant was certainly no materialist, and yet in this entire development in the direction of positivism he played a part, he formed a phase and—at a higher level than ordinary materialism—a factor. For his restricting the possibility of knowing to ordinary experience, his rejection of metaphysics, his making things-in-themselves unknowable and his denial of the possibility of contact with another world (although this other world existed for him), all this fitted in perfectly with the spirit of the day. To put it another way, he was the spokesman of this spirit. To this extent Kant, at his own philosophical level, is a typical philosopher of the radical Enlightenment, who banished so many traditional ideas and—let us not forget it—rightly made short work of many kinds of superstition. But the question is: did those thinkers go too far? It might be that in various respects the Enlightenment cast away the good with the bad. Consequently, there were all kinds of reactions to this casting away. In the first place, the philosophers who came after Kant, the so-called German idealists such as Fichte,

Schelling and Hegel, took little heed of Kant's ban on occupying oneself with metaphysics. It is true that about 1840 a time came, when people were inclined completely to reject their speculations, too, with a *Begriffsdichtung* (conceptual poetry)!, so that materialism was almost entirely the order of the day, but later in the nineteenth century in a different respect various "back to" movements followed, first a "back to Kant" and later a "back to Hegel", etc.

As regards our present subject, one may consider first the rise of spiritualism—usually at an unscientific level—, later the founding of the Theosophical Society and above all the institution of the British S.P.R. and the serious research of several generations of parapsychologists as the manifestation of a reaction to this elimination of the possibility of the occurrence of unusual phenomena and to the denial of all contact with forces of a different nature, especially those from another world. For many this obviously went too far. Certain phenomena continued obstinately to point in another direction.

The roots, the beginning of the positivistic tendency in the Modern Age, must be sought fairly far back. Confining oneself to the obvious, to what is directly given, implies a rejection of the more distant, which before had formed a continuous whole with the obvious. This might be called a tendency towards *a pregnant dualism*,[25] a swing to one end of a scale, moving away from the opposite end. Francis Bacon had drawn attention to the importance of experience and of the aspect of power inherent in all knowledge, but it was René Descartes who formulated and worked out dualism. What is usually called his anthropological dualism is the sharp distinction which he made between thought or the spirit on one hand and matter and the physical in its extension on the other. This distinction, this dualism thus runs right through man, in his opinion. In a certain sense Descartes built further on Thomas Aquinas, who assigned a purely spiritual existence to souls and to the angels, whereas many other Christian theologians had assumed for these two categories either a subtle material envelope, or at least a material foundation, a materia spiritualis.[26] In Descartes' anthropological dualism such assumptions are completely impossible, and in this way a motif, hylic pluralism, which has played a major role in the history of human thought,[27] is expelled from European thought, apart from certain undercurrents of no great size, and conversely this thought was alienated from this motif. This anthropological dualism—which interacted with the above-mentioned positivistic tendency—had a great effect on Western thought, but in a different way. It is obvious that, if it is seriously considered, the belief that mind and body mutually influence each other, the so-called influxus, which Descartes still accepted, is not possible either. Bearing this in mind, the Spinozistic parallelism, which teaches that the two series, that of thought and that of extension, constantly run side by side, means an improvement. But in itself psychophysical parallelism is equally the expression of a dualism: according to this view the events of the one series and those of the other series never interact. However, the more the two series or the two substances are made independent of each other, the more the possibility arises of dropping one of them entirely. Descartes had already declared animals to be automata or machines. Small wonder, then, that Lamettrie, in his *L'homme machine* (1748), extended this to man. The greater and the more fundamental anthropological dualism is at the beginning, the more easily radical materialism follows in its train. Then only matter is regarded as real, and the mind is viewed only as an epiphenomenon. Now all this has its effect on the present topic. Balthasar Bekker already denied on Cartesian dualistic grounds the possibility of the devil or spirits intervening in our world, although he believed in their existence. The fundamental controversy between Kant and Swedenborg must be regarded in the same theoretical light. Swedenborg claimed that he was in contact with spirits in practice, Kant denied the possibility of contact between the two worlds on theoretical grounds. Like Bekker, he still believed in the existence of that other world—the subject, he says, is a member of both[28]—but between them, between our ordinary knowledge and another, there is a fundamental barrier. In philosophical terms Kant expresses this as follows: our knowledge has to confine itself to phenomena; noumena, things in themselves, are unrecognizable. Surely it can be seen that this gives voice to, is a consequence of, anthropological dualism in close contact with the positivistic tendency to confine oneself to what is first given: he, Kant, bears passionate witness to his belief in the chasm running right through man. In his view man may be a citizen of two worlds, but his right hand does not know what his left hand is doing.

It is time for Western thought to abandon the point of view of anthropological dualism and to make a clean sweep of its far-reaching consequences. Now in various contexts an anti-Cartesian tendency is already finding expression. For instance, the emphasis put from various sides, including existentialism, on the unity of consciousness or soul and body is symptomatic of this.[29] It seems as if the spirit of the day is already changing, and not only in the field of theoretical philosophy, turning away from a pregnant dualism, from the obstinate inclination to see everywhere sharp, irreconcilable contrasts: between nations and races, between Occidental and Oriental thought, between men and women, between classes and between religions, or between the subdivisions of religions. In our context this means that it is no longer considered necessary to regard matter as the only real thing, as materialism does, or to regard the mind in this light, as psychical monism[30] and related points of view do. But then a similar development is to be expected in the contrast between Kant on the one hand and Swedenborg or parapsychology on the other. It was a pregnant dualism that Kant displayed, when he tried to confine the possibility of knowing to ordinary experience. The proofs which parapsychology has assembled in recent decades with regard to the reality of phenomena such as telepathy and clairvoyance, christened ESP, extrasensory perception, by Rhine, mean that another experience besides the ordinary one exists. The latter may very well appear to be *continuous* with ordinary experience, although this still involves many kinds of problems. The theory of the foundations of parapsychology will have to concern itself with these problems. Further, one must of course make a distinction between the results of parapsychology concerning ESP, which are in a much more advanced stage of certainty, and parapsychological research into survival of man and the possibility of contact with those who have passed over. The latter research is rather having its ups and downs. However, in order that investigators may devote themselves freely to research they will have to detach themselves in both cases from anthropological dualism. Kant, following in the footsteps of this doctrine, asserted that *in principle* contact with another world was not possible. In his rejection of Swedenborg's pretensions in the *Träume* he scored a victory, generally speaking, for his day and for the nineteenth century.[31] One of the reasons for his victory, which led to a rather generally unfavourable opinion of Swedenborg,[32] was that Swedenborg in particular did not have a very strong case as a seer, which Ernst Benz also states.[33] Accordingly the problem of contact with other worlds was set aside, as Kant desired. But development has not stood still. Modern parapsychological research has come, and its factual results demand a philosophical background with a place for them.

All these problems can be solved only by a reorientation. This presupposes abandonment of anthropological dualism, which demanded or brought in its train respectively a preoccupation with the obvious, the tangible and the visible which was useful in its day, but which was in essence one-sided. If this one-sidedness is realized, if the urge of the Enlightenment to choke off all kinds of things that at bottom might well be true is realized, then the gateway is opened to new fruitful research; then tackling certain problems is not made impossible in advance.

One of these problems is that of man's survival after death. Now we do not wish to assert that this is a problem of supreme importance. The philosophers and others who say that *aeternitas*, eternity which can already be experienced even here and now, is more important than *sempiternitas*, continued existence in time, are in our opinion right.[34] And yet the problem of survival is of a certain import all the same. It really is a *testimonium paupertatis*, or to put it another way a disgrace, that man in his pursuit of knowledge has as it were halted here and not yet made greater progress. Research into physical space may boast of great results; it is at present in the limelight. In Antiquity it was assumed that there was a fundamental difference between the sphere of the heavenly bodies and our sublunary world. This dividing line has long been discarded. And yet it is forgotten that this different world of the Ancients had another meaning besides that of the visible heaven of the stars, viz. that of the abode of the departed. They used to regard these two meanings as identical. In our time the second meaning, under the influence of positivism, has been almost entirely expunged, or at least very much disregarded. Not entirely, for the various religions, insofar as they are still listened to, have kept alive belief in this other world, which may very well be located in a direction or dimension quite different from that of ordinary physical space. But one also encounters widespread scepticism about life after death. We remember a prominent and in himself likeable speaker at a cremation ceremony who said: "The departed is now in a land about which nothing can be known". With these words he obviously voiced a general conviction in liberal religious circles. But this seems to us to be a sad dilemma: either to accept dogmatically or to reject sceptically. In wide circles the question of survival after death is hardly regarded as a real problem any longer. And yet it makes sense to pose this problem, also apart from motives of personal concern and fear. Parapsychology will have to work at a solution to this problem. Who knows, perhaps this science will steadily increase in importance. My teacher Heymans (who was, by the way, also interested in these problems) gave an academic address in 1909 on *The Future Age of Psychology*. Now if one compares the interest in psychology, the number of psychology students and the place given in society to this subject then, over fifty years ago, and nowadays, it can be seen that something of this prediction has certainly come true. Who knows, it may be possible some day to speak in analogous fashion of an age of parapsychology. This will depend in the first place on the actual workers in the field of parapsychology. Factual results will be decisive. And if the work does produce such results, the consequence will be that a counterbalance is formed in this respect (something that is needed in other respects, too) against one-sided concentration on this ordinarily visible world, with its striking technical achievements and its increasing prosperity.

But this will not only be a matter for actual parapsychological research; there is also a task for philosophy to perform here. Philosophy can facilitate acceptance of the results of parapsychological research by causing changes in view of the world to be accepted. Its task is in the first place negative: it can point to the one-sidedness of this positivistic concentration on the obvious, as a result of which unusual phenomena are often declared impossible in advance of their occurring. Further and in particular, it can point to the incorrectness of that form of anthropological dualism which found favour with Kant: of the restriction of knowing to ordinary experience, which he considered necessary and which, if it were correct, would make a priori contact with another world, with a *Jenseits* or a hereafter, impossible. The philosopher can go still further into detail by combating the distinction which Kant makes between phenomena, which can be known, and noumena, or things-in-themselves, which cannot.[35] When doing so various motifs advanced by Kant, such as that of synthetic judgments a priori and their origin in the subject, may very well prove to be of lasting value. Only Kant ascribed this origin to the wrong subject.[36] If it is associated with the one real Suprasubject, a series of problems changes accordingly. One of the consequences is, for instance, that *another dividing line* is drawn, no longer one between the physical on the one hand and on the other hand the psychical or the soul, plus the spirit, which is lumped in with the former, but between the homogeneous and continuous physical *and* psychical on the one hand and the one spirit or the suprasubject on the other.[37] Then anthropological dualism will have been defeated on this important point, with the result that the sharp dividing line, the barrier, between the physical and the psychical and between this world and the next will disappear. And then, at the same time, a basis will have been laid for overcoming Kant's negative point of view with regard to the possibility of seership and for surmounting the mistrust with which Kant and others view the occurrence of those unusual phenomena to which parapsychologists draw attention.

NOTES

[1] Address delivered at the Annual Meeting of the Netherlands Theosophical Research Centre at Amsterdam on October 13, 1962, and to the Philosophical Association at The Hague on November 14, 1962.

[2] Cp. "Moet het Kantianisme verlaten worden of voltooid?", *Mens en Kosmos* 1953, IX, 2, p. 73 *seq.* and in *De Grondparadox e.a. v.e.e.*, p. 79 *seq.*

[3] Cp. C. D. Broad, "The Relevance of Psychical Research to Philosophy", *Philosophy* 1949, XXIV, p. 291 *seq.* (Cp. *Tijds. v. Parapsychologie* 1950, XVIII, p. 114 *seq.*)

[4] See for instance E. R. Dodds, "Telepathy and Clairvoyance in Classical Antiquity", *Journal for Parapsychology* X, p. 290 *seq.*

[5] Prince August Wilhelm of Prussia (1722-1758).—For these cases see C. D. Broad, "Kant and Psychical Research", *Proceedings S.P.R.*, Part 178, 1950, and in his *Religion, Philosophy and Psychical Research* (1953); E. Benz, "Kant und Swedenborg" in *Swedenborg in Deutschland* (1947), p. 241 *seq.*—The letter to Charlotte von Knobloch appears inter alia in I. Kant's *Werke* (Cassirer edition) IX, p. 34 *seq.*

[6] *Werke* IX, p. 38.

[7] *Werke* II, p. 329 *seq.*

[8] *Op. cit.*, p. 261 *seq.* The letter to Mendelssohn is dated April 8, 1766 (*Werke* IX, p. 55 *seq.*).

[8a] A new edition of these has been edited by T. Weismann, Pforzheim 1964.

[9] In Pölitz edition, p. 257.

[10] *Vorlesungen Kants über Metaphysik aus drei Semestern.* Abhandlungen der phil.-hist. Classe der Kön. Sächs. Gesellschaft der Wissenschaften XIV, VI.

[11] Cp. E. Benz, *op. cit.*, p. 267; C. D. Broad, *op. cit.*, p. 126, cp. p. 150.

[12] "Träume" (*Werke* II), pp. 367-368.

[13] *Op. cit.*, p. 237.—It may be adduced against this that after the *Träume* of 1766 and before the *Kritik der reinen Vernunft* of 1781 Kant wrote the *Dissertatio* of 1770, in which a less sceptical attitude towards metaphysics again comes to the fore (cp. R. Falckenberg, *Geschichte der neueren Philosophie*, pp. 303-304). But the *Träume* may nevertheless have represented one of Kant's decisive initial approaches to criticism.

[14] Cp. E. Benz, *Emanuel Swedenborg* (1948), p. 308.

[15] *Träume*, pp. 352-353. Incidentally, in the *Träume* passages also occur which anticipate the postulates in the *Kritik der praktischen Vernunft*, for instance at the end (II, p. 390). Thus in the *Träume* one already encounters not only the restriction to ordinary experience (*e.g.* II, p. 384), but also the compensation thereof.

[16] *Werke* III, p. 543.

[17] II, p. 351.

[18] *Werke* III, p. 543. This passage is retained by Kant in the second edition of his main work.

[19] H. Vaihinger, *Kommentar zu Kants Kritik der reinen Vernunft*, II[2], p. 431, note 1; 512.

[20] *E.g. Die Philosophie der Mystik* (1884, [2]1910).

[21] *Op. cit.*, p. 431, note 1.

[22] *Op. cit.*, p. 234.

[23] It is true that Kant himself all the time considers a possible *intellectuelle Anschauung* alongside the *sinnliche*, but from the beginning he interprets the former as so heterogeneous that he cannot but reject at once continuity and contact between the two.

[24] Cp. *Ochêma* I, p. 56.

[25] Cp. *Tweeërlei Subjectiviteit*, p. 442.

[26] Cp. *Ochêma* I, p. 69.

[27] Cp. *Ochêma* I, *passim*.

[28] See above, page 13.

[29] Cp. C. A. van Peursen, *Lichaam-ziel-geest*, p. 32; 143 *seq*.—In our opinion it is in keeping with this idea of unity that, if anything survives, it must also have a (subtle) material side.—For the anti-Cartesian tendency see for instance *Philosophy in the Mid-Century* II, p. 93.

[30] Psychical monism, like psychophysical parallelism, proceeds from a dualistic conception.

[31] Romanticism, incidentally, was of a different opinion.

[32] See above, pp. 10-12.

[33] *Emanuel Swedenborg*, p. 574. In his visions he apparently did not always make a sufficient distinction between their contents and his own opinions and wishes.

[34] Herman Wolf, *Onsterfelijkheid als wijsgeerig probleem*, p. 248 *seq*.—J. Krishnamurti also does not wish to lay any stress on survival. Cp. *De Grondparadox e.a.v.e.e.*, p. 109.

[35] Cp. inter alia *Variaties op één en meer themata*, p. 36 *seq*.

[36] Cp. inter alia *Drei Vorträge über Philosophie und Parapsychologie*, p. 30.

[37] Cp. *Tw. Subjectiviteit*, p. 290 *seq*.

II

THE IMPUTATION OF EVIL[1]

In Theosophical literature one encounters views about evil and sin, about the criminal and his treatment in prison, about gossip and repentance, which diverge more or less from current ideas.

Gossip, for instance, is much more strongly condemned than is usually the case. This attitude, frequent enough in Theosophical writings,[2] probably reaches back to an early paper by Madame Blavatsky: "Is Denunciation a Duty?"[3] According to her, in certain special and rare cases it may be one's duty to reveal other people's evil, but on the whole she protests vehemently against the habit of talking over the shortcomings of others, unthinkingly, by way of conversation, and of passing them on.

In regard to repentance a saying, said to have been uttered by a Master of Wisdom, is often quoted: "The only repentance which is worth anything is the resolve not to do it again."[4] Generally speaking there exists in Theosophical circles no very favourable opinion with regard to awareness of sin, the realization of one's shortcomings and guilt, which are so outstanding in Christianity. In the Liturgy of the Liberal Catholic Church—founded under Theosophical influences—allusions to one's sinful condition are avoided, as well as the self-humiliating *Mea culpa, mea culpa, mea maxima culpa* of Roman Catholic Mass.[5]

There is a tendency to stress the good, the positive, everywhere, and to pay as little attention to the negative as possible.[6] Man is a being evolving through many lives; there is hope for him, if he is of goodwill; he need not implore admission to an everlasting heaven or fear damnation to everlasting hell.

No wonder that the problem of the criminal has always commanded the attention of Theosophists. They keenly disapprove of the prison-system,[7] and try to do something in the prisoner's interests.[8] Criminals are either younger souls living in surroundings that are strange to them or men whose development has been lop-sided.[9] Capital punishment is repudiated unconditionally.[10]

With regard to crime itself it is clearly said to be a *disease*.[11]

Concerning evil Dr. Arundale writes: "Difficult as it may be to believe, there is, when one comes to analyse motives and actions, no such state of consciousness as that expressed in the term 'wickedness.' Ignorance, yes; weakness, yes; but nothing more"[12]

All these utterances seem to be connected in some way, though all is not yet quite clear. As a rule, as soon as disease enters into the matter, one no longer thinks of guilt. Is the criminal then not guilty at all? If no wickedness exists, can nothing be actually imputed to a person at all? Do not wrong actions get off far too lightly thus? And does not even the distinction between good and evil lose its sense in that way?

We shall go into these questions in this paper and we shall do so by enlarging on a treatise entitled "A Perspective of Ethics," which we published in the Dutch *Journal of Criminology* of April 1939.[13] On the one hand we shall give a short résumé of that article, while on the other hand we shall elaborate the subject in the light of Theosophy.

Every man has his own *character*. What is meant by that term "character"? Apparently it is used in different ways. There is, first of all, the *type* of character, with which characterology deals. There exist various classifications of the types of character: "cyclothymes" and "schizothymes" of Kretschmer, the eight types of the Dutch psychologist and philosopher G. Heymans; the ancient division into melancholics, sanguinics, phlegmatics and cholerics; the Theosophical classification according to the seven rays; the astrological types, etc.

In all these cases what is meant is psychological type or *psychological character*. Apart from the latter, which is sometimes called *temperament*, there is, however—and this involves a second and quite different use of the word "character"—*ethical character*. One person is good, the other bad, and between these two there exist various gradual transitions.

Ethical character is an established concept of western thought. The German philosopher Kant sharply distinguished between character and temperament. Notably Schopenhauer has clearly pronounced that every human being possesses an immutable ethical character of a certain colour, or mixture of good and evil. This has been the ruling conception of the Occident ever since. Heymans also tacitly presupposes this in his ethics. His successor, Professor Leo Polak (1941 †) says it quite clearly: every man has his innate and immutable character, *i.e.*, a personal preference for certain reactions, which is in contrast to and independent of all that may happen to him or reach his consciousness: outer world and circumstances, course of life and environment. This character can be base or nobel together with every possible temperament.[14]

One thing, however, is obvious: this western theory of an immutable ethical character does not tally with the eastern and Theosophical doctrine of the evolution of the soul through many lives on earth. According to this doctrine man develops continually also with regard to his moral qualities; taught by experience he constantly changes for the better.

It is true that one might observe that these changes take place by leaps and bounds, as according to this very doctrine the experiences of one's most recent life on earth are transmuted, in the hereafter, into qualities, which will reveal themselves in the next incarnation. In this way ethical character might remain unchanged throughout one particular life. As a matter of fact, there exists a certain relative permanency of character in a certain individual, who, generally speaking, behaves fairly uniformly during one given life—for which period the saying of Goethe can often be applied: *Du bist am Ende wer du bist.*[15] But is this relative immutability also an essential permanency—even merely for one life? On the contrary, it is fairly obvious that that change of character which in the hereafter causes one to be reborn with different qualities, already starts down here. Probably in a certain number of more or less rare, but in themselves important cases, that change is already accomplished in the life on earth. If there be an evolution of the soul, the earth is not the last place in which definite progress can be made.

So one is compelled, from a Theosophical standpoint, to look out for a theory concerning ethical character different from that of essential immutability. Exactly such a theory we have set forth in the paper mentioned above—though our reasons for doing so were not only of a Theosophical nature.

In that paper we followed up distinctions which are already being made in ethics, such as the reasons, on certain grounds, for lessened imputability. A common distinction in ethics is the difference between the wrong deed and the intention. It has not always been made—in the Middle Ages one punished animals and even inanimate objects for what they had brought about—but nowadays the distinction is universally accepted. If one hurts a person without evil intention, one is certainly responsible for the fact and its consequences, but the deed is not (unless recklessness or imprudence supervenes) morally imputed to the person concerned. When a child in its ignorance, for instance, causes a person pain, one does not say (without more ado) that it appears from that act that the child has a bad character. In other words, though a wrong action has been committed, there are various circumstances preventing one from reaching a conclusion with regard to the character of the doer. In such a case there is simply no room for "moral imputation."

Heymans gives in his *Einführung in die Ethik* a series of examples and cases of this. Bad education, reading and intercourse, temptation and provocation, irresistible emotion and *primary function*[16] cause displacement of the motives represented and engender an at least partly lessened imputability.[17] A person who kills another *need* not be callous; he may even, in general, be compassionate; certain ideas have in that case, however, prevented the motive of compassion from exercising its influence. A debtor who forgets to pay, owing to a grievous personal loss, may very well as a rule be a dutiful person. One does not know, in such cases, in what way the persons concerned would have reacted to such a motive as pity or duty, independent of that particular circumstance, and it is only thus that the moral character of an individual can be judged.

The reasons for diminished imputability form a curious case. They go rather far and their limits are not very sharply defined. The person himself, or others near to him, often know much better how he came to perpetrate his actions than outsiders, who, moreover, not infrequently judge unkindly. It is contended, therefore, *e.g.*, by Professor Heymans' other successor at Groningen University, Professor H. J. F. W. Brugmans (1961 †) that one should be very careful in applying imputation. But "the world" often forgets even that obvious ethical law that one should know the motives before judging at all: the same action can spring forth from very different motives. It seems that among burglars the fact whether a comparatively wealthy or a poor man is robbed is certainly taken into account. But if one really starts from the idea that the former may be ridden of his "too much", an *intellectual* motive enters into the matter which, according to the official rules of ethics, influences the *moral* imputation in the same proportion. We do not by any means contend that burglars should have their way; we shall go back to the point of the consequences of the *action* as regards legal responsibility and penal law later on; we are now dealing with imputation: with the conclusion that can be drawn about the moral *character* of the doer. It appears from the foregoing that this imputation is at any rate in many cases very difficult, even according to current ethics.

Following up such conceptions the writer then took a big step in the above-mentioned essay: he raised the point whether factors might not be working which prevent, in *all* cases of evil, imputation to the moral character of the doer. If he is right, nobody would have a moral character somewhere between white and black; on the contrary *everybody* would have, despite his wrong *actions*, an identical and essentially *good* character—in complete accordance with the Theosophical teaching that good is *latent* in every man.

This point of view should be elaborated in various directions. What is its significance in the science of ethics; what is the nature, then, of those factors which prevent imputation in *all* cases, though the reverse may seem true; what are its consequences for the persons concerned, for public opinion and for criminal law?

First of all: one might be of the opinion that, thus, the moral distinction of good and evil would disappear. However, this cannot be maintained. To elucidate this we must go somewhat further into the matter. The writer's thesis is that imputable evil is, in fact, never committed, as there are always circumstances preventing imputation, not only partially but wholly. That does not, however, in the least alter the fact that one is able to *realize* that, *if* those circumstances did *not* obtain, and somebody were nevertheless to act in the same way, that then imputable evil would be committed. In other words, *theoretically* and *hypothetically* evil can be very well known and imputed. Moreover, good *can* be imputed. In this way the distinction between good and evil does not lose its significance at all; what is actually committed is however only *hypothetical evil* (hypothetical as far as the imputation of the intention and not as far as the action is concerned). All this being an illustration of the old saying that one should hate sin but love the sinner. In this case one is *allowed* to love him.

The whole situation may become clearer, if we draw a parallel to the field of theoretical judgments. In connection with the latter it is always assumed that every human being has ultimately the same mechanism of thought. With regard to the very divergent views of men one attributes this fact to the varying data and premises, from which the judgments start: if data and premises were the same, every one would arrive at an identical conclusion. Sometimes, here too, a seemingly different mechanism exists, as in the case of primitive men and lunatics. But the example of the sufferer from paranoia who, starting from the premise that he is persecuted, quite normally argues further, makes it likely that the difference does not lie so much in his thought-mechanism as in his starting-points. One also assumes with regard to the thinking of the stupid and backward that, if they could only imagine the issue, they would arrive at normal conclusions. Theodore Lipps sums it up in this way: Wrong thinking is incomplete thinking.[18]

Neither is it possible with regard to theoretical judgments *to err intentionally*. *Another* person can see that, if someone holds that $7 \times 7 = 48$, he errs; the person concerned, however, will, at that moment, *bona fide* believe that to be true. Parallel to this truth that no one errs on purpose intellectually, Plato already raised the point whether, with regard to moral or practical judgments, it would not be the case that *no one acts wrongly on purpose:* "Oudeis hekon poneros." [19]

If that is so, however, the questions arise as to why that is not more generally accepted; and what the factors are which prevent imputation also in those cases in which it is now usual to impute.

For most people are inclined to grant that a person who is thrown off his balance by strong momentary impressions or by strong emotions, may perform actions which do not tally with his general conduct, which he condemns strongly afterwards, and which cannot be called typical of his moral character. But doubt arises when it is maintained that not even a premeditated wrong action can be imputed. The intention, the *dolus*, makes all the difference between homicide and murder, which latter is punished far more severely. The miser or the blackmailer are not under the influence of impressions of the moment.

To *prove* that in *all* cases factors are operating which prevent moral imputation will, without any doubt, be difficult. Professor Heymans, who read the treatise *A Perspective of Ethics* before his death, wrote to the writer that he acknowledged plainly the *possibility* that the main thesis of it, namely, that only hypothetical evil is committed, may be right, adding that he of course whole-heartedly wished it to be so, but that in his opinion this had not yet been proved for all cases. Nevertheless the writer insists that some considerations can be pointed out making it likely—yet apart from other more distant reasons—that it is as contended. It is usual, for instance, to consider overwhelming emotion as a factor for lessened imputability. An example of Heymans runs that a person owing to grievous loss cannot bring himself to pay his debts in time. But what if the idea has indeed arisen in him, without, however, (as it is sometimes expressed in ethics) having been able to unfold its true motive-power? Then the circumstance of being aware of it, or even the premediation is already in evidence—but imputation does not seem to be possible.

Now all the common vices, also the long-lasting, such as greed, etc., are accompanied by emotion. The same applies to passion. Passion has two sides, one being emotion, and the other judgment. Passion attributes an absolute value to a part of the not-Self—while in truth the Absolute is only present in the One Self. Various religions and doctrines of salvation have emphazised that it is a delusion to imagine the Absolute as residing in the not-Self—a delusion which can be removed by insight, insight, not of the lower mind, but of a deeper, intuitive understanding. However that may be, as *judgment* that delusion can, again, not be imputed. And emotion is already considered as working in the same direction.

We believe that, along such lines, one is not so far from proving or making it probable that there are *always* factors acting which prevent moral imputation.

Considerations of a different and more general nature concur to strengthen this surmise.

Love has always maintained the same view, be it especially *with regard to certain persons*. It seems that the ability to see the *Perspective of Ethics* varies. Love for a particular person has again and again induced the lover to be convinced that all the evil in the person loved was merely external and incidental [20]—in contrast to the hasty judgment of "the world" which is so inclined to condemn. Maybe that saints can realize the same with regard to many persons; that it is true from an absolute and all-embracing viewpoint—such as God's—*for everybody*.

Conversely, this doctrine, that only hypothetically imputable evil exists, throws light on many Theosophical utterances. *This* is the reason why there is "no wickedness" (G. S. Arundale). This is also why—in addition to the power of thought—gossip, the unnecessary repeating of other people's shortcomings as if they were essential and permanent, is so objectionable.

Awareness of guilt and sin, useful to a certain extent, in order to realize the evil that—illegally, but not immorally—has been *done*, should not be exaggerated and should certainly not be carried so far that one considers oneself and others to be inherently, immutably and incorrigibly bad.

For the same reasons one can speak of crime as a disease. Yet wrong actions do *not* get off too lightly, for, in the first place, one can *see* that, if they were performed *without* the circumstances that prevent imputation, they would be very serious. Secondly, they remain in themselves serious, as they infringe the objective state of things. At the same time the doer is entitled to compassion and help.

In this way a strong tendency which has long existed in the Theosophical movement is theoretically established step by step.

One may still ask whether the viewpoint of the *Perspective of Ethics* does not entail great disadvantages or even dangers.

For it might be inferred that nothing whatever matters now, as it would be impossible ever to commit imputable evil.[21] In this connection we may recall that suburban gentleman's saying: "*We* have an excellent parson; he allows us to do anything!" Asked how this was meant, the answer was that according to this clergyman everlasting hell did not exist. His hearer was not slow with his inference. In other words: if people *want* to misunderstand that is their business.

One may point out, in view of such tendencies, that the evil that is *done* (though it may not be imputable) retains its full significance. The law (not only of the State) has been infringed, damage has been caused, and one shall have to atone for that, either by repairing the damage immediately, or by a mutation of his chances and opportunities in a future incarnation. With regard to several aspects of practical life it does not, moreover, make so much difference, whether *evil* is imputed, or whether a person shows certain *psychological* weaknesses, which are not morally imputable:[22] when choosing one's staff and when making many other decisions one will take it just as much into account.

One may yet maintain that a danger lies in the assertion that even premeditated evil actions cannot be imputed—in connection with the idea that they could not have been avoided. Now with regard to the criminal, scientists usually agree with the latter; insofar as more normal cases are concerned, one should consider the following. There exist, apparently, *various kinds* of evil that are done (but which cannot be imputed). A simple case is the wrong done out of ignorance, as when a child hurts somebody. At the other end of the scale there is the evil proceeding from a lasting disposition, which used to be imputed. Generally speaking, evil actions are of *two* kinds: in the first place those with regard to which it suffices that the doer's attention be drawn to it, so that the action ceases. In this case mere intellectual insight is sufficient to effect a change. In a somewhat broader sense, many influences of *milieu* and, in general, carelessness—failing "secondary function"[16]—of the individual belong to this kind. Considerable improvement can be attained in this field by education, change of environment and training. Heymans' opinion is even—without yet accepting the *Perspective of Ethics*—that the purpose of moral struggle and of moral education is not so much the transmutation of the person's character, as the development of his repressed but still existing moral inclinations.[23] This task and this possibility remain in any case, as a large field lies fallow for self-training and improvement of environment.

Apart from this some dispositions are in evidence which used to be, but, according to us, cannot be imputed on closer inspection; which cannot be altered in a twinkling by simple effort and insight, but which probably *can* be transmuted in the long run, by a changed intuition. The sharp distinction between these two kinds of perpetrated evil can only further the results of moral struggle in either of these two ways.

With regard to the latter kind one can yet maintain that it may prove dangerous to state that evil is done out of a disposition that cannot be swiftly changed, and which still cannot be imputed. But every one knows that something like that exists: these are exactly the actions and inclinations with regard to which the people concerned remain deaf to all arguments and exhortations. By setting forth a theory about this fact, one does not stimulate it, as the world has made the whole matter plain enough to the people concerned, as it is. And if anyone be so foolish as to confuse this situation with the evil resulting only from ignorance and carelessness, and which can be relatively easily altered, it is again one's own fault.

On the other hand, if it be true that not even those more serious dispositions are imputable, while they can be changed in due course, how important it is, then, for the people concerned, that the condemnation of their deeds does not exceed certain limits! How much dejectedness and despair has been caused, far more than the necessary disapproval, by all those judgments which proclaim: *you are irrevocably and inherently bad!* Humanity is, as a rule, very cruel in such things. No wonder that the remaining good in the person concerned perishes, whereas it should form the starting-point of their uplifting.[24] If our argument is correct, then that remaining good is essential: the evil, though it may be persistent, is accidental. The world in its prevailing attitude often behaves, however, as if the evil were inherent and typical, and as if at the same time such a person actually could not do any good. As a result the reaction is that he becomes quite cynical and incredulous—there is no hope for him anyway.

Here lies a task for Theosophy, which is so often uttering words of encouragement. It should go on proclaiming that sin is unreal and transitional; that not the evil actions and vice, but the extant and essential good, the existing virtues, should be emphazised.

Inferences from the above can also be drawn as regards the treatment of the criminal and penal law. The legal dilemma has always existed as to whether one should punish by way of retribution—*quia peccatum est*—or only to prevent a recurrence of the sinning by the delinquent, or by other people who should be deterred from imitating him: *ne peccetur*. If the *Perspective of Ethics* be accepted, there can be no longer any question of punishment of the "evil will" by way of retribution. Neither can the value of deterrence be very high, either in principle or in practice. But the State has to take measures all the same: for the betterment of the criminal and for the protection of society. In jurisprudence one usually distinguishes between "punishments" or "penalties" and *measures*. In the case of "measures" one has abandoned punishment or retribution on principle. The *Perspective of Ethics* implies that the criminal will no longer be punished; "measures" only will be taken with regard to him.

A tendency in this direction has already obtained for some considerable time among criminologists. They do not agree, however, on all points. Some of them stick to the demand for retribution. Others meet with the following difficulty: how can a *moderately* serious offence be imputed and punished, while with regard to a really *serious* offence, certain psychologists spontaneously declare: "he is a born criminal, one can see that his decision was no longer free, it would not do to punish him." The *Perspective of Ethics* is able to solve this difficulty. A more serious offence, of course, entails greater guilt than a minor one; if imputation were possible at all, the former should be imputed to a greater degree. Various schools realize—apart from the *Perspective of Ethics*—that imputation with regard to many serious criminals is not admissible, though their *actions* may be bad enough. This attitude should be extended in the direction of the less serious offences, which, by the way, should also be imputed—though in a lesser degree—were there in that case, too, no factors operating which prevent the imputation of evil. The difference is that the less serious cases are not at all hopeless: here changes can be effected by education, by emphasizing the positive qualities in the person concerned, and by the efforts of the offender, who can acquire a different disposition, either fairly swiftly or gradually. In this way the *Perspective of Ethics* removes the seeming contradiction between the attitude towards a minor and that towards a serious offence.

But why are some thinkers so convinced as to the idea of retribution? It is as if the idea of retribution—that pain should follow an offence, as much as joy should be the reward of good actions—is deeply rooted in the human mind. Now such tenacious notions—whether one calls them "innate ideas" or otherwise—often appear subsequently to be well-founded. This might also be the case with the idea of retribution. But it occurs that one has associated such notions *with the wrong point*. The wrong direction one has taken would, in this case, constitute *punishment by man*. If, however, one accepts the eastern idea of Karma: that pain and pleasure in certain conditions, *e.g.*, a certain life on earth, are *the result* of good or bad actions under other circumstances, *e.g.*, a former life, then the *verworrene Gedanke* (to speak with Kant), the confused idea of retribution proves to be sound after all; it appears to be not without reason so deeply rooted in us. But retribution is, then, not man's business. One is reminded of the ancient text: "To Me belongeth vengeance and recompense" [25] Erringly man has punished, whereas he ought to have supported and helped. How one can give up punishing out-of-principle without the disinction between good and evil becoming meaningless—this the *Perspective of Ethics* teaches us, setting forth the impossibility of moral imputation, the identical good character of every man, and the hypothetical nature of the evil that is done.

Besides, neither does God or Nature punish in principle by means of Karma. Pain and pleasure are distributed according to strict justice: where an offence has been committed, balance must be restored. For the same reason the intention or disposition (save insofar as it is itself an action) is not the criterion of Karma, but the action or deed, so that wrong actions, according to these presumptions, though they may not be imputable, will, nevertheless, always have karmic results.

In the Middle Ages animals and even inanimate objects were punished for what they had brought about. To such an extent did deeds serve as the criterion—while men felt themselves called upon to carry out the punishment. By and by one distinguished action and disposition—the deed as such and its meaning and intention. In the same degree one attributed less personal guilt—though in law the factor of the *action* has always thrown weight into the scale. The latter will have to remain so: remember the duty of indemnification. With regard to condemning one's neighbours less and less personally, considerable development can, however, still take place. Manners and customs are continually being mitigated. Only a century and a half ago lunatics were chastised and exhibited. The religious demand to love one's neighbour, to hate sin but love the sinner; certain opinions in criminological circles; Theosophical utterances disapproving gossip and too severe punishment—all these indicate the same trend, a trend towards the further evolution of the attitude as regards guilt and imputations. The *Perspective of Ethics*, which says, and carefully explains why, the reasons preventing imputation should be extended to all cases of evil done, can provide a theoretical foundation for all this.

May the tendencies towards this, that in practice already exist in various *milieus*, gain strength. May all these factors co-operate to prevent or abolish abuses, to encourage and reform offenders, to further and uplift suffering and imperfect, yet evolving, humanity.[26]

NOTES

[1] See *The Theosophist*, July 1941 (LXII, 10), p. 289 *seq.*; *Variaties . . .*, p. 79 *seq.*

[2] See A. Besant and C. W. Leadbeater, *Talks on the Path of Occultism*, p. 280 *seq.*; G. S. Arundale, "Criticism," *The Theosophist*, April 1933, p. 62: *idem*, *S. Michael's News*, July 1936, p. 147; G. Hodson, *The Theosophical World*, Dec. 1937, p. 291.

[3] *Lucifer*, III, p. 265 *seq. The Theosophist*, July 1923, p. 373.

[4] Cp. A. Besant and C. W. Leadbeater, *Talks on the Path of Occultism*, p., 73.

[5] Cp. C. W. Leadbeater, *The Science of the Sacraments*, p. 75 *seq.*

[6] Cp. G. S. Arundale, *Gods in the Becoming*, II, p. 551: "On Weakness."

[7] Cp. A. J. St. John, "Prison Reform," *The Theosophist*, Jan. 1920, p. 337; Serge Brisy, "The Prisoner," *The Theosophist*, April 1936, p. 46; *The Theosophist*, April 1933, p. 53.

[8] Cp. a.o. C. Jinarājadāsa, "A Talk to Prisoners," *The Theosophist*, Oct. 1929, p. 21; *idem*, "The Power of God in Man," *The Theosophist*, Sept. 1934, p. 619; B. Poushkine, *Prison Work on Theosophical Lines* (Adyar Pamphlet); Serge Brisy, "The Prisoner," *The Theosophist*, April 1936, p. 46; *idem*, "Behind Prison Bars," *The Theosophist*, March 1939, p. 472.

[9] A. Besant, *The Changing World* p. 89; *A Study in Consciousness*, p. 183.

[10] *The Changing World*, p. 95, etc.

[11] C. W. Leadbeater, *Talks on "At the Feet of the Master,"* p. 595; cp. *Talks on the Path of Occultism*, p. 868.

[12] *You*, p. 47.

[13] "Een Ethisch Perspectief," *Tijdschrift voor Strafrecht*, XLIX, 2, p. 147.

[14] W. J. Aalders, a.o., *Causaliteit en Wilsvrijheid* (Groningen 1936), p. 23.

[15] "At the latter end you are who you are."

[16] In Psychology the "primary function" of the contents of consciousness is their immediate influence when in the centre; the "secondary function" is the influence of those contents that are almost below the level of consciousness or that are subconscious. The person whose "primary function" is strong will readily give in to the impressions of the moment, while a strong "secondary function" causes the whole of his past to influence his present—often even too much, so that this person is then not capable of adapting himself sufficiently to the demands of the moment.

[17] *Loc. cit.*, § 12.

[18] *Die Ethischen Grundfragen*, p. 66.

[19] Cp. *Hippias minor*, 376B; *Laws*, 731, 860; *Timæus*, 86 E.

[20] Cp. C. Jinarājadāsa, "Men and Women—Real and Ideal," *The Theosophist*, June 1939, p. 260 *seq.*

[21] If one wants to prove the possibility of doing wrong by purposely removing something, one would not succeed; for the action would be in itself an offence, (as I have never denied), but imputation to one's moral character would again be impossible, as the person concerned would have been impelled by an intellectual motive: that of proving the said possibility.

[22] A person, as a rule, belongs to a more or less definite psychological type showing certain positive qualities and—as *les défauts de ses qualités*—certain weaknesses entailing the danger of some kind of trespass. Thus the thoughtful person will be economical and run the risk of becoming miserly; he who has a strong will will be energetic and plucky, but perhaps callous and cruel; and so on with various complications.

[23] Cp. *Einführung in die Ethik*, pp. 299, 305.

[24] One is reminded of the Roman Catholic Church refusing Holy Communion to anyone who is (not a member etc. and) not without sin, while the Liberal Catholic Church—since *God is Love*—admits every one who approaches the altar reverently. It is true that the L.C. Service has General Confession and Absolution, while on the other hand R.C. Absolution is not meant to cover a lifetime, but still there is a big difference between the two views. And the viewpoint of the L.C.C. excludes the idea of eternal hell: in the Creed included in the Shorter Form of the H. Eucharist it is said: "We believe . . . that all His sons shall one day reach His Feet, however far they stray."

[25] Deuteronomy 32:35.

[26] Notwithstanding, in the human individual there lies a strong tendency to

take punishment in his own hands. Extending this to Society, this may very well be in its interests. The human individual is, after all, the "infrasubject", and Society a product of infrasubjects. The infrasubject, as such, is *not* the "suprasubject" or God. The power of the infrasubject to know, for instance, is necessarily fragmentary and limited. In the same way, the human ability to forgive might be restricted. Nevertheless, it may be very useful to raise the problem, whether the character of human individuals is permanently immutable and the same and, therefore, sometimes good, sometimes bad, or, perhaps, changeable and inherently good.

III

THE HOME[1]

It is good to be at home again after a holiday.

The house is the physical resting place of the family; such is also his room to the bachelor.

It is, as if one is nowhere so rooted as there. Here attention can wander from without to within. Here it is comfortable; everything has been arranged according to one's own taste. But even worn-out things are familiar.

One person experiences much more strongly this attachment to a starting-point in space than another. Moving is to him a punishment. He needs even temporarily a spot where he can cast his anchor. Others easily flutter from one place to the other. It is, as if in the one individual age-old trees, in the other butterflies and birds have left their traces. Of the ancient elements in the one Air, in the other Earth seems to dominate.

Man's life consists of constantly being chased. *Repos ailleurs*, "Elsewhere there will be rest", ran the motto of William the Silent's right-hand man and friend Marnix of St. Aldegonde. Nevertheless many people stay somewhere for a relatively long time: in the home and in the *Heimat*. For others there is no such thing: they are seeking a new fatherland. Sooner or later comes the moment for everyone, when the home is broken down, also in that narrowest sense: of the breaking up of the body, the earthly tabernacle.

So there is a parting that means dying a little, and a dying that is no more than a temporary parting.

Because of the insecurity of the earthly dwelling, man has always looked round for another, more permanent, spiritual abode.

The house of God has thus become to him a dwelling in a deeper sense. In his incorrigible limitedness he again thought he could find it in an earthly edifice. Still, his realizing that he is more at home in the sanctuary, at the altar of Him, Who showeth Himself upon a thousand altars, is deep and sincere.

"Our hearts are ever restless, till they find their rest in Thee"—the community repeats it again and again after St. Augustine.

The true resting-point of the cosmos lies in God Himself. All temporary resting-places are but reflections of that one deepest centre of gravity. In the same way all the smaller selves reflect but the One Self.

As we are all of His flesh, the true dwelling of all of us lies in

God Himself. As we are, however, at the same time small, failing human beings, we also have a temporary home all the time, or we are longing for one.

It is good preaching about the eternal dwelling, apart from which there is no peace. In the meanwhile one's earthly abode and tabernacle can be pleasant and cosy.

When the hurricane rages and houses tremble in their joints, when bombs fall, and walls collapse, then we truly remember our eternal home.

September 1939

NOTE

[1] See *The Liberal Catholic*, May 1940.

IV

THE TWO SOPHIA'S OR THE RELATIONSHIP OF THEOSOPHY AND PHILOSOPHY[1]

Philosophia ancilla theologiae—Philosophy is the handmaid of theology: thus a thinker of the Middle Ages, Petrus Damiani (1007-1072) expressed what according to him was the right relation between philosophy and theology.[2] In these centuries, not all have given proof of a similar lack of appreciation for philosophy, but in those times it was generally accepted in Europe that philosophy had to take second place as well as be a servant to theology.

One can raise an identical problem as to the relationship between *philo*sophy or "love for wisdom" in general, and *theo*sophy, usually rendered as "divine wisdom".

Before going into this problem in principle, we wish to find out how this relation is in practice; how, for instance, leading theosophists think about philosophy; what philosophizing theosophists there may have been; the study of which subjects philosophy and theosophy apparently have in common and towards which philosophical trends theosophists are attracted. However, we shall have to do all this very quickly.

Firstly, it is striking that—whereas a leader like MR. C. W. LEADBEATER apparently took little interest in philosophy[3]—DR. ANNIE BESANT positively appreciated philosophy and its function. This appears, for instance, from her address on *Philosophy or God manifesting as Understanding*, the third of six lectures given at the opening of the Brahmavidyashrama in Adyar in 1922.[4] There, she gives a very right definition of philosophy as "the definite intellectual attempt to understand the universe in which man finds himself as a part."[5] Also, her positive attitude re philosophy is constantly coming to the fore in her interest in Indian philosophy.

Whereas DR. G. S. ARUNDALE was as little interested in philosophy as Mr. Leadbeater, we have a series of pronouncements on the subject from MR. C. JINARĀJADĀSA. Only, they rather diverge. In the Foreword to the second impression of the collective work, entitled *Where Theosophy and Science meet*, he writes that in due course other works such as *Where Theosophy and Philosophy meet* will have to be published.[6] However, he has many faults to find with today's philosophy.

According to him, in the field of metaphysics one finds oneself occupied by "matters not worth discussing".[7] Today's philosophy is "purely an intellectual analysis of mental processes".[8] What he is especially nettled at, is that the study of philosophy seems to have so little influence on the formation of character; in ancient India and in Greece this was different: there, purification of the emotions was the first requirement for the study of philosophy.[9]

Meanwhile, there is one philosopher for whom Mr. Jinarājadāsa has a great admiration; this being Plato, who—according to Mr. Jinarājadāsa—is all too little studied by theosophists. He was a social reformer and actually he was neither a philosopher nor did he have a system [10]—statements which we would rather not support.

Mr. Jinarājadāsa also wrote about Schopenhauer.[11] Those three thinkers: Plato, Schopenhauer and Bergson, usually are warmly welcomed by theosophical authors.

It lies near also to ask ourselves which significance is attributed to philosophy by H. P. Blavatsky in *The Secret Doctrine*. However, this question is not easily answered, since *The Secret Doctrine* has so little system. As far as we can see, no definition or appreciation of philosophy as such is given anywhere, even if many scattered remarks are to be found in its pages in connection with various philosophers and their ways of thought, in comparison with the esoteric doctrine. In these sundry remarks, again Plato and Hegel seem to be liked best.

Various individual theosophists have occupied themselves in a more systematic way with philosophy. Among these, I may recall, for instance, Bhagavan Das (1869-1958) and Douglas Fawcett (1866-1960) and among the Dutch M. W. Mook (1876-1926) and J. J. van der Leeuw (1893-1934). Apart from his greater works, Bhagavan Das gave a lecture at the Philosophical Congress of Bologna in 1911 on the subject of *The Metaphysic and Psychology of Theosophy*, later published as an Adyar Pamphlet.[12]

Mr. Fawcett has been a member of the Theosophical Society between 1885 and 1891, therefore not for a very long time. Yet it is apparent that his later philosophical work was influenced by theosophy.[13]

Of the, at least in Holland, lesser known authors we should not forget to mention Miss Charlotte E. Woods, who a.o. wrote about "The Self and its Problems" (1922), as well as Miss H. S. Albarus, who did not deny her German background in a series of well-considered philosophical articles in *The Theosophist* [14] and elsewhere. B. L. Atreya, professor at the Hindu University of Benares, who (as far as we know) never was a member of the Theosophical Society, contributed an—in our opinion—rather vulnerable paper to *Where Theosophy and Science meet* about *Philosophy and Theosophy.*[15] In a somewhat wider sense we must, of course, mention DR. G. R. S. MEAD (1863-1933), who was in the first place a classicist and a student of comparative religion and as such was constantly brought into contact with the problems especially of the philosophy of the Ancients.

As regards Holland—in this country a rather vivid intercourse between philosophy and theosophy has taken place. On the one hand, Professor BOLLAND (1854-1922) criticized theosophy,[16] whilst accusing my own teacher at the University of Groningen, Professor HEYMANS (1857-1930)—who himself thought of theosophy as "obvious superstition"[17]—of theosophical sympathies in connection with his psychic monism, of which Bolland said: it is "New Knowledge, Ancient Wisdom".[18]

On the other hand, we can point to a series of Dutch philosophizing theosophists. It should not be forgotten that MR. J. D. REIMAN JR., in the years, when—mostly on his instigation—the International School of Philosophy was founded near Amersfoort, was a theosophist, as well as his wife, and the leader of the lodge of the Theosophical Society in Amersfoort.[19] Dr. J. J. van der Leeuw has, especially in his *The Conquest of Illusion* (1928), treated, or at least touched upon, a large number of philosophical problems. A clearly philosophical theosophist was Mr. M. W. Mook; see his *Hegelian-Theosophical Essays* (1913) and various other, small pamphlets of which he was the author.

For that matter, a curious thing has occurred with the relationship between Theosophy and Hegelianism. Some people appeared to have had an understanding of both, even though some of them started by being theosophists and ended by being Hegelians, then rejecting theosophy as a preliminary stage.[20] The now rare "panphilosophical magazine" *Licht en Waarheid*, originally contained much theosophy; finally, it was converted into the purely Hegelian magazine: *Denken en Leven*. One of the most important Dutch Hegelians after Bolland, JACOB HESSING (1874-1944), since 1932 a special professor in Hegelian philosophy at Leyden University, has been a theosophist for some time—apparently under the influence of W. Meng. Even in later years he sometimes mentioned the saying "Satyānnāsti para dharma", which—so he said—should be ascribed to the Emperor Akbar and which according to him might be used as a device for any system of philosophy.[21]

Being a theosophist, one can apparently go in various philosophical directions!

In India, it is apparent that theosophy is strongly influenced by that Indian philosophical trend or *darshana*, the Vedānta. Dr.

Besant called the Vedānta "the greatest of all systems."[22] Nevertheless, putting the One Self into the centre has also been criticized: thus, one cannot get rid of the (lower) self and one is kept imprisoned within the subjective. Western idealism, even all great philosophical systems, are so very sterile and subjective, so they said.[23] We disagree with this viewpoint. It may be true that theosophists have, in their meditations, to a too large extent identified their own ego with the Self. This, in our opinion, does not detract from the significance of that one Self. Dr. Besant was quite right to agree with the Vedānta doctrine.[24] However this may be—apparently it is possible to render theosophy in different ways in philosophical ideas. Also, it is very useful that we are free to do so and that not merely one philosophy—like Thomistic philosophy for Roman-Catholics—is considered to be the leading system.

On the other hand it can be said that there exists, nevertheless, some affinity or relationship between theosophy and certain philosophical trends. In the first place it can be established where this affinity is *not* given: for instance, with regard to materialism and positivism. The theosophist is unable to accept the idea of visible matter being the end, the truest reality. Neither does he agree with positivism, which only reckons with the—physically or psychically—tangible, thus never reaching the *spirit*. Nor can the theosophist be content with an extreme, or left existentialism, which teaches life to be absurd. No, on the contrary, he is in constant search of a *background*, which is not given, from which that which is immediately given, life and the world, only receive their meaning and can be derived.[25]

Thus, a theosophist naturally turns in the direction of a *spiritual* philosophy, which places spirit in the centre, whether he looks for it more especially in Hegelianism or in the (to our opinion not yet sufficiently known) spiritual existentialism as found with LOUIS LAVELLE (1883-1951) or in the Vedānta or in a Western counterpart of the Vedānta, called "absolute idealism" by the German philosopher Nicolai Hartmann.[26]

At any rate we can observe that theosophy and philosophy partly meet with the same problems. To mention some of them: the relationship between mind and body, or between the psychical and the physical, between spirit and matter; the bearing of intellect and intuition; the meaning of the rational and the irrational; eternity and time; freedom; the polarity of individual and society, etc.

If this be so, if philosophy and theosophy partly deal with the *same* subjects, then, only the more, the question arises of their exact and essential relationship. Now we wish to go into this. We must find an answer to the question: Which of the two is the highest?

Which of them has the last word? Is the one the servant of the other?

Here, however, we must make a restriction. If we want to compare theosophy and philosophy, then only theosophy is at stake, as far as it is part of the process of thinking. It is most probable that theosophy has yet other aspects or functions. Thus, the question boils down to this: If we put philosophy, which certainly is a matter of thought, and theosophy, insofar as it is thinking, beside one another, which will then be the strongest of the two; which one will turn the scale?

It has always seemed to me that in order to find an answer to questions such as this one, it is necessary to start from the difference between theory and practice and to point out that there exists also a *practice of thinking*. Pure theory is a rather late invention. Primitive peoples occupied themselves with all kinds of things: building of bridges, healing of the sick, etc., long before drawing up beautiful and complicated theories on how such things ought to be done. That is not something to begin with. So it is with thinking itself. Man is already convinced of the truth of various teachings about himself and his constitution, about the cosmos and its various parts, without being able to give exact proofs for these opinions.

Afterwards, these opinions often appeared to be quite wrong, but even so, I think that the anticipation of pure and established theory has an important as well as a lasting function. Otherwise, no result could ever be obtained; we have to start with various suppositions, the truth and the utility of which may eventually appear later on.

This does not only bear upon the best ways of building; it also bears upon general theories concerning the world and life and the task of mankind in them. Man is continuously confronted with decisions: to which purpose will he educate his children; how should the state and the community be run and ruled; on what grounds punishment is given?

Man cannot wait until every field has been exactly covered by science or philosophy. Therefore, he begins by accepting as correct on grounds of intuition a whole complex of opinions or teachings with regard to such general matters, and to act accordingly. This is both necessary and useful. For these complexes of provisionally accepted doctrines the term "ideologies" in the better sense *(Weltanschauungen)* should be used. This term, which as such might also be used as a synonym of philosophy, is often used in this narrower sense; of complexes of general teachings about mankind, life, the world and the reason for the existence of the world, as yet unproved, but nevertheless accepted with a strong conviction.

There is no one—except perhaps some dry and inactive Dr. Cipher (to quote a well-known Dutch novel) who is able, as a matter of fact, to do without such an ideology. Man is forever bothered by decisions; he has to cut the Gordian knot, if only about the problem for which political party to vote!

In my opinion, the religions also come under the head of "ideology" as regards their complexes of doctrines, for instance Roman-Catholicism, Protestant Fundamentalism, Islam, etc., etc. Their followers will not agree with our definition of as yet un-proved, but useful teachings. According to them, they teach *the truth*, even before it has been confirmed. It is revealed truth." Dogma", originally only meaning opinion, principle, took the special meaning of an a priori established doctrine, being dogma in a narrower sense. According to me, this implies an overestimation of the task of ideologies, so that immediately the problem arises of how, for heaven's sake, all these, often contradictory complexes of dogmata can all be true at the same time.

Also, the contents of the various doctrines coming under dogma, vary often: as scientific research makes progress, many ideas are abolished which formerly were accepted as established truths. Undoubtedly, however, religions in the sense of ideologies do have the function of giving guidance and security in life. Not all ideologies are dogmatic. Liberal Protestantism, for instance, does certainly accept more than is exactly proved, but it does not *require* acceptance. There are also negative ideologies. The Freethinkers, for instance, put freedom of thought before everything else and they will have none of religious teachings or dogmata. The question is, of course, whether they themselves are completely free of all dogma: their freedom of thought often amounts to "at no cost belief in God", that is to say, to a dogmatically accepted atheism.

There exist many ideologies, especially if we also take into account the smaller groups, such as those of the Spiritualists, Mormons, Christian Scientists, and so on. It is obvious that Modern Theosophy, founded as a Society in 1875, is one of them. When envisaging as an outsider, that is to say as a student of comparative religion, those groups—one can observe all kinds of them, whether they be called sects or trends or ideologies—they all bring their own outlook on the world, thus satisfying the human need of a survey and hold on life. In the meantime, each of them (and sometimes violently [27]) claims that his system is the truth. Insofar as the teachings of the various ideologies contradict one another, they cannot possibly, however, be true at the same time.[28] It is likely, that each time a different aspect is brought to the fore. These aspects might eventually supplement one another—the one system might then be more suitable for one type of person, the other for another type of person, without the contents of the systems necessarily contradicting one another—, but that is something which is not easily accepted: one's own system contains the complete truth.

There seems to lie a great task for an ideology which brings these various aspects to the fore, seeing them as parts of a greater whole, whilst pointing out the common background of the various religions.

Each one of us has to make his own choice of ideology, unless he automatically accepts that kind with which he has been brought up. He, who chooses the ideology of Modern Theosophy, will then, as happens elsewhere, be guided by partly explicit, partly intuitive considerations.[29] With the latter, the intuitive considerations, we can again observe the practice of thinking: which starts from that which is not yet fully proved.

Let us now have a look at the counterpart: *philosophy*. One of the questions repeatedly asked here, is that of the relationship between philosophy and science. We all agree, I think, that science really has the purpose to promote freedom and certainty of thinking, accepting only strictly proved results. It is true, science does often start from certain premisses or axioms, but this then forms a new problem: science at any cost wishes to prove (or at least to know exactly) where they come from and how far they hold good. These are really philosophical questions. Now then, is philosophy part of science or something else? That is partly a matter of definition. Sometimes one speaks of *Die Weltanschauungen der grossen Denker* (the ideologies of the great thinkers), for instance the philosophy of Schopenhauer, then meaning ideology in the above-mentioned narrow sense of a coherent complex of assumed, but not quite proved teachings. However, we prefer to give a more severe definition of philosophy. For philosophers equally strict requirements of exact demonstrability and objectivity should be expected as for science. In that case, however, philosophy also comes under the head of science; she is the summary and the crown of science, but she remains part of it. All those un-proved systems, then, are cases of ideology in the narrower sense, of provisionally accepted teachings, which eventually may be proved later on.

Thus having defined theosophy and philosophy, the former as an "ideology" and the latter as a part and the crown of science, what conclusion can then be drawn as to their interrelation? Which of them has the final word? To this question, according to us, the answer ought to be without reserve: philosophy. According to theosophy, this *has* to be so. This is the result of the fact that theosophy is a liberal spiritual trend. The Theosophical Society wishes to be a society of *searchers* for truth; when becoming a member, acceptance of a credo is not required; at the most, its members should agree with the first aim concerning the formation of a nucleus of Brotherhood.

I remember my first meeting with Mr. W. B. Fricke in 1918 who at that time was a prominent member of the Theosophical Society, Netherlands Section. Then, he said to me: "We believe in reincarnation, but always remember, if we find something better, we shall accept that."

In practice, one may sometimes meet rather orthodox theosophists who swear by certain teachings or pronouncements. What, for instance, is to be found in the *Mahatma-Letters*, is regarded by them as strictly and completely true. According to me, however, even these letters are a result of the viewpoint of a certain circle in a certain period.[30]

Meanwhile, there is no better proof for the undogmatic character of the Theosophical Society than the motto which is put round the seal on all its publications: *Satyān nāsti paro dharmah*, which is usually rendered as: "There is no religion higher than truth". Truth, as found by unhampered thinking, which especially occurs in science and her part and crown, philosophy, is *eo ipso* higher, of more importance than any religious consideration. By that motto, the liberal, non-orthodox character of theosophy is officially indicated. A stronger contrast to *philosophia ancilla theologiae* cannot be thought of; theology, in this case theosophy, is definitely not the handmaid of philosophy; it is rather the reverse. In principle, one cannot, accordingly, acknowledge a "double truth"; free thinking, philosophy and science carry off the palm in a conflict.

Theosophy, however, also contains various detailed teachings. If, for instance, reincarnation, therefore, is not a dogma, if there are so many more teachings, such as the existence of higher planes and subtle bodies and the Path of Initiation, all this has not been strictly proved and yet we often talk about it. This should be regarded thus: that it all comes under the heading of "ideology" in the typical sense of that which one intuitively feels inclined to accept, whilst awaiting a further scientific or philosophical proof (for instance to be found, perhaps, in parapsychology for the theory of reincarnation[31]).

In the meantime, one might consider the following too. On the one hand, it is dubious, as said, whether theosophy is only a matter of thinking; on the other hand, as also mentioned before, one is confronted by the choice of an ideology. This choice will be the more easy and justified, if the contents of the ideology concerned are clearly outlined, logical and deep. According to us, these contents should be full of meaning, have philosophical significance and they should also be liable to being *understood*.[32] The unconditional acceptance of a certain, traditional religion on the grounds of the message of a certain leader, important as he may have been, to our opinion can never satisfy these demands.

Now, whe have looked for a formula of what theosophy in an embracing sense really is, having already expounded such a one elsewhere.[33] Very shortly, one might say that modern theosophy is a *synthetic* movement, a movement aiming at synthesis, integration, unity, be it unity in diversity. This aiming at unity or integration can then be specified according to the direction in which it is expressed, in the first place either inwardly or outwardly.

Inwardly, the aim is directed at God or the One Self, resulting in: 1) reflection on, and finally contemplation of God or the Divine, i.e., seen from the outside, highest philosophy, respectively deepest (free) theology; 2) personal surrender and devotion towards God or mysticism; and 3) a gradual real union with God, or yoga.

When, however, man turns *outwards* in his desire for unity, other cultural values come into existence. When he tries to understand and explain the world or plurality, science and the rest of philosophy, the philosophy of plurality, are born. When man tries to create certain unities within the world, art and ceremonial magic originate. When he aims at unity in the practice of daily life, a fraternal loving or harmonic community on a smaller or larger scale comes into existence.

Unity *between* the various cultural values is a goal too; for instance harmony between art and religion, between science and brotherhood, between science and religion, where, again, we should find unity in diversity, that is to say, the autonomy of these cultural values should basically be retained.

This wider definition of what theosophy is, includes also a description of an *ideal theosophy*, of theosophy as an ideal. This amounts to a realizing the proper signification of this ideology and, the more this signification is evident and worthy to aim at, the more people will associate with it. From this ideal theosophy, theosophy brought into practice should be distinguished, which is a movement since 1875, one among many other movements and ideologies. That is, however, a very common thing; that which is formulated as an object, always goes deeper and is more beautiful than when it is put into practice. If, for instance, we read the programmes of political parties, they all are equally or almost equally fine. Apart from the objects, it will also depend from the realization of the same, whether one is willing to remain a member of a certain movement. If the gap between the aims and their realization becomes too wide, many turn aside. We think, however, that no discussion is necessary about the importance of pure, deep and understandable formulas of the aims to be reached.

We can make some more remarks about this definition of "ideal theosophy". Its contents are very broad. Fundamentally, ordinary philosophy and science do also come under its heading: they aim at unity as regards knowledge! Also mystical, social and oecumenic aspirations come under the heading of ideal theosophy. Then, should we say that this definition might be *too* wide? This is not so, according to us, for nowhere else but in the Theosophical Society this ideal of a universal synthesis, integration or unity in diversity and brotherhood is so explicitly expressed. It is an ideal worth aiming at.[34] We shall, however, frankly have to acknowledge that many aspects of it are already pursued and also realized elsewhere. It will not do to regard the whole complex of deeper philosophy or the progress of science as part of the activities of the Theosophical Society, founded in 1875! One might go on giving such examples.

However, there should be a special relationship between this ideal theosophy and the modern theosophical movement—otherwise, there would not have been so many enthousiastic theosophists in the course of time. In our opinion, this special relationship is, that nowhere else that many-sided synthesis (for instance with regarding to the so important idea of brotherhood) is so explicitly formulated,[35] and that also in certain other respects the connection between the purpose of unity and its realization comes expressly to the fore here.

To all probability, it will particularly be possible to enter the Path of Initiation via the Theosophical Society. On the other hand, we shall always have to bear in mind that the Theosophical Society is one of a series of idealistic, religious and humane movements, each of which aims at an ideal lying beyond its reach. As regards this Path of Discipleship and Initiation, we cannot believe that this might *only* be entered via the Theosophical Society. If that which is indicated here, be as important and central as is assumed, it should be possible to find it elsewhere, too; for that matter, it existed already long before 1875.

Therefore, I do not deem it correct to mention "self-exploration, the experiencing of everything as a Mystery" as typical for theosophy or the Theosophical Society and to regard everything else as immaterial, so that, for example, the Theosophical Research Centres would not even be allowed to call themselves "theosophical".[36] Yes, of course, experiencing the Mystery—either in the direction of thinking, in the form of what we call the "fundamental paradox", or in the direction of the experience of mystic unity—is the most important, the deepest, or—so to speak—the "only needful" thing.

Let us hope that this mystery is especially experienced by theosophists; yet, it is likely that others, too, experience it, for instance in Zen Buddhism.

Actually, this is also the viewpoint of J. Krishnamurti: the most necessary thing is awareness. Everything else does not matter, is of secondary importance. For J. Krishnamurti, everything else is so very accidental, that he does not wish to occupy himself with it at all: neither with philosophies, nor with religious organizations, nor with religious ceremonies, and so on.[37] However, not everybody can take such a high, exclusive viewpoint all the time. Even if Mary be basically right as regards the one needful thing (Luke 10:42), the sisters Martha are also wanted.

We thought that the members of the Theosophical Society might exactly be those who—although acknowledging that the most important factor is self-exploration, the experience of the Mystery—will nevertheless feel called upon (as so many sisters Martha) to occupy themselves, besides that, with other things: spreading of teachings, for instance those regarding what leads up to the Path, of which that mystic experience constitutes the summit,[38] pursuing brotherhood in daily life, comparing the results of ordinary and occult research (like the Theosophical Research Centres do) and much more, consciously taking the viewpoint that, nevertheless, an organization for a spiritual purpose has its meaning and use, in spite of the dangers involved.

To our opinion, one will never be able to say that the Theosophical Society would be the *nec plus ultra* of ideologies, or, so to say, the absolute ideology. Then, one would not be liberal any more, but orthodox. However, if one wants to be and remain a member, one has to be convinced that the Society has a special task to complete. This special task is a consequence of that very broad and profound aim, such as we have tried to formulate as "ideal theosophy", theosophy as an ideal.

In the meantime, one can see various tasks for the members of the Theosophical Society and according to his range of interest and his type of person, each member will want to devote himself to some particular task.

With regard to our subject: "theosophy and philosophy", we can now ask ourselves: might there perhaps also be such a special task for a certain group of theosophists within the boundaries of philosophy? Philosophy is, as we have seen, the summary and the crown of human thought, of the search for truth. On the other hand, theosophy—although it is more, since it also aims at unity or integration in other, for instance practical respects—at any rate also has a theoretical side, concerned with ideas: it teaches, it wants to promote insight. Thinking is, in any case, involved.

That such is the case, is explicitly recognized by various leading theosophists. They say that there are different roads leading to the summit and to liberation of the self, and in this connection jnāna-yoga, bhakti-yoga and karma-yoga (i.e. yoga or unification through knowing, devotion and acts) are mentioned. Mrs. Besant, for instance, writes about this distinction in *The three Paths to Union with God*[39] and also in her booklet *Hints on the Study of the Bhagavad-Gītā*[40] she speaks about this jnāna-mārga, this *road of knowledge*. In the fourth chapter of this treatise, she quotes the Gītā about this yoga of wisdom and discernment, which a.o. comes clearly to the fore in its fourth and thirteenth chapter.

Now, philosophy is—or at least ought to be, for there are philosophers who have given up this ideal—the summit of human thinking, reflection on the profoundest problems, such as a.o. the relationship of man, the individual subject, to the foundation of the world, the One Self or the Absolute. Apparently, human thought here reaches its boundaries and can now only move forward in a faltering manner, only "know quand même, nevertheless".[41] But thus, the situation becomes even more interesting, in spite of the risks involved. Now it is obvious, that this jnāna-yoga, the mārga or the path of knowledge to reach the Supreme, is connected with these most profound problems of philosophy. In so far, theosophy should also have a special relation to these deep realms of philosophy.

If one does not have in mind modern theosophy, dating from 1875, but the older, historic theosophy,[42] then one can observe that this connection between theosophy and profound philosophical thought has often existed. One may think, for instance, of Plotinus' philosophizing about the One, Plotinus, who, on the other hand, also knew religious extasies. Jacob Boehme, too, used to ponder on the paradoxes in the relationship of God and the creation or multiplicity: concerning, as he called it, "the contrarium in God".

One can say that this jnāna-mārga has been followed by many thinkers: in India by Shankara in his doctrine of Advaita and by many others; in the Western hemisphere, for instance, by Spinoza, who wrote about the *amor dei intellectualis*,[43] the intellectual love for God by man, in which God also loves Himself.

More on the religious side, there have been the Gnostics, who—however motley in their various trends—all put understanding, reflection on the foreground, whereas Christianity as a whole can rather be called bhakti-yoga than jnāna-yoga.

Mysticism also assumes different forms, devoted mystics apparently practising bhakti-yoga again, whereas the so-called "cool mysticism" of—for instance—Meister Eckehart rather takes the side of jnāna-yoga. Much jnāna-yoga is also evident in Buddhism with its supposed atheism, or rather its negation of a personal God; and J. Krishnamurti teaches—without *wanting* to be a teacher!—the same non-devoted, but cool, conscious realization of the highest, which apparently is comparable with "satori" of the Zen-Buddhists. Here, throughout "deprojection" is apparent, in contrast to the projection of God or gods, to whom one is lovingly devoted.[44]

So, on the whole there is enough to point out, coming under the nature of jnāna-yoga, this way of deepest knowledge. Now, we wish to ask the question how things are in the Theosophical Society. There the jnāna-yoga is explicitly acknowledged as shown above.[45] Yet it appears to us that there is no reason for enthusiasm. There are some philosophers who are in good favour, so to say, with the members of the Theosophical Society, such as Plato, Hegel to a certain extent, and also Shankara and his Vedānta, but one is not much, or not very intensively, occupied by jnāna-mārga. This may have special reasons. One can say that in the past, there was more studying in the Theosophical Society. The necessity of this seems to have taken more or less second place nowadays. Probably, there have been two causes for this: 1) the significance, given to intuition and 2) the viewpoint of J. Krishnamurti.

As regards intuition: among the philosophers popular with theosophists, also HENRI BERGSON (1859-1941) should be made mention of. Against the dry and rigid intellect he sets intuition as the function capable of experiencing pure duration, *l'élan vital* and creative activity. He is one of the so-called philosophers of life, who really renounce understanding in order to stop at experiencing, which, in our opinion, amounts to a sceptical attitude with regard to the possibilities of thought. Here, too, much use is made of intuition and too little use of the intellect, whereas, according to us, merely at one special point, namely understanding the "fundamental paradox", the intellect fails us and only the pure intuition of each one of us can bring relief.[46]

According to us, theosophists have made too much fuss of this conception of intuition by Bergson and some others. Probably, the cause of this has been that there are also theosophical teachings about the succession of races and about the development of various functions within these races. The fifth race, now in existence, would especially be characterised by the flourishing and preponderance of the intellect, of *manas*. This race is succeeded by the sixth race, now coming up, in which the faculty of *buddhi*, often rendered as "intuition", will be developed. Bergson's teachings would then, so to speak, anticipate this and be a sign on the wall.

Dr. Besant, however, somewhere makes an important remark.

She says that she does not like the term *buddhi* for intuition, since there exists an intellectual intuition totally different from the intuition of buddhi, which is self-realization. There is, according to her, a stronger relationship between emotion and buddhi than between manas and buddhi.[47] In other words: a distinction should be made between two things: between the intuition of buddhi, a direct evaluation of things, and the intuition of manas, where intellect by itself comes to intellectual intuition or intellectual contemplation *(intellektuelle Anschauung)*. Then, there are two roads that can be followed: They who already at this moment want to become aware of buddhi,[48] take a different direction than those who—starting from the prevailing race—want to reach its summit, where intellect reaches its boundaries and realizes the fundamental paradox. The latter is the typical road of knowledge. Jnāna-mārga forms the immediate lengthening-piece of the fifth race. The point is not a mere rejection or renunciation of the intellect, but a step by step and conscious abolishing of the intellect by itself, as also Hegel wanted to do.[49] In other words: the highest can also be reached starting from thinking itself: it is aware of its abolition in an "understanding, nevertheless". This is quite different from merely leaving and outlawing intellectual thinking. In this way one can, therefore, judge favourably the significance of thinking and, accordingly, it is not right to relinquish study because of intuition.

For, even although thinking reaches its boundaries somewhere, none the less all kinds of preparatory stages belong to it. One can see the whole development of thinking as leading towards that purpose. For this, however, all sorts of trends in the history of philosophy have to be studied and commented upon. So, study is necessary as well as the whole apparatus of knowledge, including a good documentation.

As regards, secondly, J. Krishnamurti, we have pointed out in a study that his rejection of philosophy, too, includes a philosophical standpoint.[50] We consider his "cool-analytical" point of view to be a form of jnāna-yoga, of the road of knowledge. This is apparent from the importance given by him to "awareness". That he wishes to have so little to do with all those preliminary steps, for instance the refutation of other viewpoints, is typical for him and for his desire to concentrate on the only necessary thing: the immediate self-liberation. That need not, however, prevent others from occupying themselves with that preliminary work and its intellectual elaboration.

So there are various reasons why the road of knowledge has to a certain extent taken second place in the Theosophical Society. Still, this is to be regretted. Even if for many this road is too complicated or too subtle, it should nevertheless be there. One should not underestimate the influence of thinking, this time not as "thought-power", but as to the contents of ideas. It has so often happened in history that ideas have been submitted to a small circle at first, to gain more and more ground and becoming common property at the latter end.

In order to create a better community, that is more based on co-operation, including even the whole of mankind, it is of the greatest importance that the ideals of unity are spread, even if people nowadays are already much more prepared to accept them than some fifty years ago. We should not only voice the ideal, or express a desirability; the synthesis or integration should also possess a theoretical background or foundation. This background can in the last resort be found in the conception of the One Self embracing all and everything, in other words: in a rejuvenated Vedānta doctrine. This *can* emerge from the theosophical circle, but then it will be necessary to pay more attention to the road of knowledge.

In the *Mahatma-Letters* two different tones can be heard: a pessimistic one and an optimistic one. The pessimistic one is that it is a "forlorn hope" for theosophical volunteers to devote themselves to this cause against the multitudinous agencies arrayed in opposition.[51] The other, optimistic tone is also heard from Master K.H. when he formulates the goal as follows: "The crest wave of intellectual advancement must be taken hold of and guided into spirituality".[52] This is exactly an appeal to theosophists to play a leading part in the thought currents of the era.

How can this be possible, however, if the road of knowledge and study comes so little to the fore in the movement?

At the end of our considerations we wish to put this matter in a clear light. In the years 1925-1927, many members of our movement held great expectations of three kinds of activities that—even without precisely belonging to the Theosophical Society—yet were indirectly connected with the Adyar Society. These were: the Liberal Catholic Church, the Co-Masonry and the movement to promote a Theosophical World-University. These expectations were followed by a serious reaction, when J. Krishnamurti's actions took another direction than was expected. After the first shock had been received and digested, however, the Liberal Catholic Church and the Co-Masonry continued their course, not without success, whereas of the third movement, aiming at a Theosophical University, practically nothing has ever been heard since. It is true that it still exists as a corporate body and that as an aim it has not yet been abandoned,[53] but as a whole the plan has been put off until further notice. One reservation should be made, however. The activities in this direction are continued under the more modest name of Theosophical Research Centres. The English Theosophical Research Centre, for instance, produces excellent work, even if elsewhere the results may not be so impressive.

We will point out something else. In Holland, theosophists have the privilege to have in their midst an important international occult centre, i.e. St. Michael's at Huizen-Naarden. How fine and useful would it be, if we could, in this connection, make a start with an international theosophical university in the rather more unassuming form of a theosophical academy! DR. D. J. VAN HINLOOPEN LABBERTON, recently deceased, cherished designs in this direction in the twenties,[54] but alas in a rather rash and unfortunate manner, as was the case with his other educational projects too. It seems that since—it is a pity to have to make this statement—the interests regarding study usually come behind other things in "the Centre".[55]

Nevertheless, according to the contents, to the idea, there is space for a theosophical-philosophical school of students, which might take shape in a theosophical academy. The shining example for this is Plato's Academy itself, even if it met with periods of scepticism in later centuries.[56] In the centuries of Neo-Platonism the Platonic school then flourished in various centres: a.o. in Alexandria, in Rome and again in Athens. The influence of Neo-Platonism has been enormous: via Origen, Augustine and Pseudo-Dionysius the Areopagite on Christianity; within Islam through Arabian thinkers like Alfarabi and Algazel and also on the Jewish Kabbala. When, during Renaissance and Humanism, the study of the classics was again taken up, Platonism flourished once more with men like Pletho, Marsilio Ficino (with his Platonic Academy in Florence) and Giordano Bruno.[57] Via Boehme and Swedenborg, who had a great influence on Romanticism, Neo-Platonism is also influential in our times,[58] especially in various occult circles. The gnostic and mystic aspects of Christianity are always connected with it.

This theosophical academy-to-be should, on the one hand, have to largely include the study of *comparative religion.* In this connection, we may remember the work of Dr. G. R. S. Mead (1863-1933), who alas left the Theosophical Society at a given moment. His further work in his society and magazine, both called *The Quest,* is continued to a certain extent, also chronologically, in the *Eranos-Conferences* of Ascona, Switzerland. There, on the Lago Maggiore, a woman of Dutch birth, MRS. OLGA FRÖBE-KAPTEYN (she died on April 25, 1962), did a great work by gathering every summer during many years a number of prominent scholars of comparative religion and depth-psychologists—a.o. Dr. C. G. Jung, recently deceased—and promoting the publication of their talks each year.[59] When this institution, which might very well be called an Academy, started, it seemed as if—as a result of the cooperation of Mrs. Katherine Tingley—this work would assume a more or less theosophical stamp. In later years, Mrs. Fröbe did not, apparently, want to have anything to do with theosophy any more. However, in the excellent work done here, we find a good example of what the theological section of a theosophical academy should be like.

On the other hand, *philosophy* ought also to play an important part in such an academy. There is an important development going on, sometimes called *Revision of the Enlightenment.*[60] The Enlightenment of the 18th Century, however useful for the fight against all kinds of superstition, has, in various respects, rejected the good with the bad.

Here, Immanuel Kant also lent a hand by proclaiming the impossibility to know "things in themselves", for instance to know the world in which, also in his opinion, man survives after death. Dr. Rudolf Steiner was quite right when, in a booklet called "Philosophy and Theosophy"—dating from his theosophical period[61]—he observed that the agnosticism of Kant was very infertile: "form" (in the sense used by Aristotle) can indeed be transferred from object to subject, so that the subject is surely able to know things.[62] If, however, the barrier—supposedly existing between this and the other world—is *in principle* broken down (like various seers have already done in practice), then the whole view of the world is altered. Parapsychology, doing such useful research-work, is so very often looked upon with a suspicious eye, because people still bear the old idea in mind that there cannot be anything in the realm of consciousness other than that which has entered this realm through the *ordinary* senses. Therefore, this other world also has to be uncovered theoretically. This happens when one does not any more draw an essential dividing line between the spirit (or mind + soul) in contrast with the body, but between the One Spirit, the One Self and (soul + body, or the psychic + the physic).[63] Then there is room to also objectify the psychic worlds.[64] Thus, there is a huge task for philosophy, often connected with the idea of the all-embracing, unity-creating, One Self, which idea can have a very strong influence indeed on the entire view of the world as well as on the interrelation of men.

It has been said here, that it is useful to make these things clear. For, what do we see in practice? A small interest in philosophy and a diminished interest in study, in the "road of knowledge", among the members of the Theosophical Society. One is rather lonesome this way; one sees oneself as the voice crying in the wilderness.

Thus, one sits between two chairs: theosophists wish to hear little about philosophy and academic philosophy is only too apt to dispatch the philosophical ideas one proposes, by saying: "That is nothing but theosophy!" It is, however, self-evident that one cannot make bricks without straw and that where nothing is, Caesar looses his right.

Yet it is right to point out the possibility of such a development, of team-work in a theosophical-philosophical spirit, eventually resulting in a theosophical academy or even a university and—what is even more important—in a beneficial influence on the spirit of the era. Who knows but that a definite development in this direction through the arrival of egos with a real interest in study, with a feeling for these problems, may be expected about 1975. However, within the Theosophical Society that date has only too often had to serve as a palliative already!

NOTES

[1] Address delivered at the Annual Meeting of the Netherlands Theosophical Research Centre at Amsterdam, October 14, 1961.

[2] See F. Sassen, *Geschiedenis der Patristische en Middeleeuwse Wijsbegeerte*, 1949, p. 93.

[3] Meanwhile, there is a curious statement of his in the essay "Higher Consciousness" (in the booklet *The Monad*, 1920, p. 51): "What down here would be a system of philosophy, needing many volumes to explain it, is there a single definite object—a thought which can be thrown down as one throws a card upon the table".

[4] *Brahmavidya*, Adyar, 1923. See *The Theosophist*, April 1923, p. 31 *seq.* and *Theosophia*, June 1923, p. 77 *seq.*

[5] *Op. cit.*, p. 34, p. 79.

[6] Vol. I (1949), p. VIII.

[7] *The Theosophist*, March 1951, p. 382.

[8] *The Theosophist*, April 1948, p. 20; cp. February 1953, p. 353.

[9] *The Theosophist*, March 1947, p. 414. In our opinion this is too strongly expressed. Nevertheless, it is a fact that in Indian philosophy the practical aspect of philosophy, its function as a doctrine of salvation, has always been in the foreground. However, apart from that, what has the truth of statements to do with emotions either sublime or not sublime?

[10] *The Theosophist*, February 1953, p. 353; cp. "C. Jinarājadāsa and the Platonic View," *The Theosophist*, August 1953, p. 346 *seq.*

[11] Namely in "The World as Idea, Emotion and Will", *The Theosophist*, August 1946, p. 303 *seq.*

[12] No. 122 and 123, cp. *The Theosophist* XXXVII, 2, p. 54 *seq.*

[13] See E. Douglas Fawcett en Raynor C. Johnson, *Theosofia*, May 1958, p. 73 *seq.* and *De Grondparadox*, 1961, p. 317 *seq.*

[14] For instance "The Doctrine of the great Self in Western Philosophy", *The Theosophist* XXXI, p. 1558 *seq.*

[15] First ed. III, p. 109 *seq.*; second ed. II, p. 113 *seq.* See our review in *Theosophia*, October 1939, p. 292 *seq.*

[16] For instance *De Boeken der Spreuken* II, 912-943.

[17] "De Tijdgeest in de Wijsbegeerte", *Haagsch Maandblad*, March 1924, p. 263.

[18] *Zuivere Rede*, p. 1227 *seq.*; cp. p. 940 *seq.*, p. 1276.

[19] J. D. Reiman Jr., *Openingsrede* (Amersfoort 1916); "Rede bij de opening van het Gebouw", *Theosophia*, October 1917, p. 271 *seq.*

[20] See our *Variaties op één en meer Themata*, 1947, p. 193.

[21] In "Het ware in de philosophie van Hegel", *De Idee*, Hegelnummer, 1931, p. 78.

[22] *The Theosophist*, April 1923, p. 35.

[23] Professor J. E. van der Stok, *Theosofia*, June 1954, p. 91; *St. Michael's News*, Dec. 1952, p. 28.

[24] See our paper below: Ch. XII and "Die Fruchtbarkeit der Grundgedanken des Vedānta für die abendländische philosophische Problematik" in *Kant-Studien*, Vol. 51, 4, p. 438 *seq.* and in *De Grondparadox*, p. 324 *seq.*

[25] Cp. *Theosofie en de Theosofische Vereniging* (Amsterdam, 1960), article "Filosofie", p. 33.

[26] See *De Grondparadox*, p. 325 *seq.*

[27] In this respect, the groups that are not sceptical-cautious, but which onesidedly claim that their special viewpoint is right, have priority in practice; they form a united group, ready to make sacrifices.

[28] Concerning the concept of the One Truth, cp. *Variaties* . . ., p. 10 *seq.* and *Alg. Ned. Tijdschrift v. Wijsbegeerte*, June 1963, p. 201 *seq.*

[29] In our opinion, also information coming from trustworthy clairvoyants should be taken into account—if one wants to anticipate somehow that which in the end will be proved to the satisfaction of everyone. It is true that the statements of clairvoyants are also liable to mistakes, as the clairvoyants themselves point out, but they are better than nothing at all.

[30] Compare the discussions in the latest volumes of the *Science Group Journal*, published by the English Theosophical Research Centre, about the discrepancies between certain statements in the Mahatma-Letters and results of contemporary science. See also *De Grondparadox*, p. 307 *seq.*

[31] Parapsychologists recently pay again attention to cases of remembrance of past lives. See I. Stevenson in *Journal American S.P.R.* 1960, p. 51 *seq.* and elsewhere.

[32] Cp. the saying of Dr. A. Besant: "Give me understanding and I shall keep Thy law!"

[33] "Een ruimere definitie van theosofie", *De Theosofische Beweging*, May 1932, p. 199 *seq.* and elsewhere. See *Variaties*. . ., p. 208 *seq.*

[34] It is closely connected with the notion of *evolution*.

[35] It is remarkable that in the *Purposes* of the United Nations, founded in 1945, Art. I, 3 runs: "encouraging respect for human rights and for fundamental freedoms for all without distinction as to race, sex, language or religion". The latter part looks like an echo of the First Object of the Theosophical Society. In the Universal Declaration of Human Rights this is still more the case.

[36] Mr. A. J. H. van Leeuwen in *Theosofia*, February 1960, p. 43. According to Mr. van Leeuwen, truth has no room in universities! But what else but the search for truth is the aim there? Such a statement can only make sense, if Truth (with a capital T) is an indication of the same Mystery, like Krishna-

murti speaks of "Truth or Life or God" (cp. *Variaties...*, p. 22) and if there might be a reason to deny the significance of truth in the usual sense. Even then, philosophy might approach the Mystery within the universities, namely by assuming the "fundamental paradox" to be the highest principle.

[37] Cp. *De Grondparadox*, p. 105 and *infra* Ch. VIII.

[38] Krishnaji's comment would immediately be: "no path!" However, the others hold the opinion, though that may fundamentally be right (compare "become what you are"), that it is possible to *prepare* oneself for that experience.

[39] 1897. Dutch translation, Amsterdam 1912.

[40] 1906. Dutch translation, Amsterdam 1907.

[41] It is here, where the concept of the fundamental paradox comes in. Cp. *De Grondparadox*, p. 14 *seq.*; *infra* p. 74.

[42] For this distinction see the article "Theosofie" in *Handboek van het Moderne Denken*, Arnhem 1950, p. 753.

[43] *Ethica*, pars V, prop. XXXIII.

[44] See *De wijsgerige projectie*, Assen 1958, p. 12 *seq.*

[45] Cp. also G. Hodson, "The way of knowledge", *The Theosophist* XLIX, 3, p. 323 *seq.*

[46] Cp. "De waardering van het verstand", in *De Grondparadox*, p. 35 and elsewhere.

[47] In "Philosophy" etc., *The Theosophist*, April 1923, p. 42; 32.

[48] One may remember the preparations for the "Sixth Race" which should already be made during the present root-race according to *Man, Whence, How and Whither* of A. Besant and C. W. Leadbeater.

[49] Concerning the relationship of Intellect and Reason cp. *De Grondparadox*, p. 27 *seq.*, not forgetting the *via negativa* of theology.

[50] Cp. "J. Krishnamurti en de wijsbegeerte" in *De Grondparadox*, p. 93 *seq.*

[51] *The Mahatma Letters to A. P. Sinnett* (A. T. Barker), p. 35. A letter of 1880.

[52] "Letter to A. Besant" in *Letters from the Masters of Wisdom*, ed. C. Jinarājadāsa, first series, 4th ed. 1948, p. 111. A letter of 1900.

[53] Cp. *The Theosophist*, April 1958, p. 8 (N. Sri Ram), January 1960, p. 219 (N. Sri Ram), p. 260 (B. Wouters), *St. Michael's News*, June 1958, p. 109 (Rukmini Arundale); *The Theosophist*, Aug. 1964, p. 345 (change of name).

[54] See our "De Beweging voor een Theosofische Wereld-Universiteit", *Handboekje van de Ned. Associatie voor de Th. W. U.*, Amsterdam 1927.

[55] As in Neo-Platonism after Plotinus the theurgical-magical element came to the fore, in Huizen the interest in the ceremonial-magical moment is dominant.

[56] Carneades a.o.

[57] Somewhat later one meets in England the *Cambridge Platonists*, such as Ralph Cudworth (1617-1688).

[58] See the essay "Literair Platonisme" in *De stille getuige*, (1960) by Professor S. Dresden.

[59] In the *Eranos Jahrbücher* from 1933 until now.

[60] See "Parapsychologie als Revision des Aufklärung" by Professor G. F. Hartlaub, *Zeitschrift für Parapsychologie* IV, 2, p. 81 *seq.*

[61] Theosofische Bibliotheek no. 47, Amsterdam 1909.

[62] *Loc. cit.*, p. 27-29. Cp. *De Grondparadox*, p. 331-332.

[63] See *Tweeërlei Subjectiviteit*, p. 292.

[64] See *Theosofie en de Theosofische Vereniging* (1960), p. 34.

V

"NEARER, MY GOD, TO THEE!"[1]

When on April 15th, 1912, the steamship *Titanic* struck an iceberg in the Atlantic Ocean, sealing the fate of many of her passengers, the ship's band, as one is told, during the sinking took up the hymn "Nearer, my God, to Thee". Many a reader will remember, too, the popularity of the hymn after these thrilling events. So it became better known than ever because of the heroic behaviour of a band in a tragic hour, and of sentimental exploitation afterwards. How many people realize, however, that the first line of the hymn contains an exact *résumé*, a short summary of *the essence of all religion?*

It is nevertheless true. For in these few words two things are assumed: Deity, Who is addressed, Whose existence therefore is taken for granted,—and Man, who is addressing Him—as "my God"—,wishing to be nearer to Him, to approach Him, to become more and more one with Him. This will always be the characteristic of the pious man: that he believes in the existence of the Divine, and in the centrality of his God; and that he desires that this conviction and this experience should more and more mould his life; that the *unio mystica* with God will grow ever more real to him, will permeate his whole existence. Meanwhile things divide according to their value: there are holy and unholy things: earnestness, moral virtue, truth, beauty, peace, selfsacrifice stand nearer to the Divine, lead nearer to God than their opposites. The man who is religiously inclined strives after the former. Furthermore, certain localities or situations are understood to be nearer to God; thus it is generally held that the "beyond," the planes of existence above the physical, are nearer to God than the world in which we are living now, while as a rule the religions concern themselves with the nature of these higher levels.

Therefore the definition of religion as the endeavour to approach God does not sound so strange. Likewise if, compared with other cultural values such as art, science, concern for society and the state, it appears that religion differs from them in that it relates all to God. All the former can exist without God, divorced from religion, in a secular or naturalistic way; conversely it pertains to religion to demand that all of them will some day be related to God, to the basis of the world, to the unity of things. Religion anticipates a world, where this has been realized; where all art is religious utterance; where the peak of science is in a free theology-philosophy;

where society is a spontaneous hierarchy and so on. Insofar as religion exists as an independent form of culture in association and in contrast with other forms of culture or cultural values nowadays, it is a reminder and a partial realization of that all-embracing relationship to be.

If all this is true, there is every reason to ponder for a while that concept of "approaching God". It may be that it is precisely philosophical reflection that will prove capable of discovering some difficulty, some contradiction therein.

As a matter of fact, one can raise the question: does not God permeate the whole of the universe, every point of it, as it is? If He does, if God is present at and behind every single point of the universe, what meaning is there left in the approach to Him; why should one give oneself so much trouble therefor? Is not every point of the universe *equally near* to God? Is not all religion—approach to God—therefore really superfluous?

We do not believe that this difficulty can easily be solved. The endeavour to come nearer to God is, as a matter of fact, characteristic of religion, but yet, if one thinks it over, all approach really seems needless.

Now there are, however, other considerations in connection with the idea of God leading to a similar difficulty, *aporia* or *antinomy*. Why, one often asks, had God, Who was already perfect, to create the world? Apparently, the world apart, He is already perfect. This being so, what reason was there for creation, and what is the use of all our endeavours to improve conditions, if the whole world is in any case irrelevant, when one considers God's perfection?

We can put aside here the way in which others want to solve these problems. The way we propose to take may or may not lead to a solution, according to whether or not fundamental insolubility is held to be a solution.—One will have to consider these problems either wholly from the standpoint of Man, or wholly from the standpoint of God, insofar as it will be possible for us to put ourselves in His place. Now it is obvious that the complaint concerning a contradiction is a typically human complaint; our intellect thinks according to the laws of logic (A = A; A = non non-A etc.), and these laws belong peculiarly to man; that is to say they serve to put order into the data of this manifested world, of the world-in-plurality. Because of the fact that, as a rule, our thinking—always connecting more than one term with another—moves always within plurality, it is to be seen, whether these laws can still be applied to the subject, that has Himself posited them and the whole of plurality: to the "suprasubject" or the One Self, in which we all—we, the "infrasubjects" or the many selves—participate.[2] From the fact that we form part of it, we are able in a way to reflect how all looks as seen from the standpoint of the suprasubject; but we are not able to solve in the ordinary way the problems that arise here for our ordinary human intellect, which can at most establish that its ordinary laws are here no longer applicable; that, while within plurality there can be no contradictions: A =non non-A, etc.—if there are, a fallacy has been made in the argument—,here, on this level, non-equivalency necessarily enters. And it is never possible to get rid of it, — so much so, that we realize ourselves incapable of eliminating it in principle, though there may be no fallacy in the argument. Now this is what we have called elsewhere "the fundamental paradox": the unremovable contradiction consisting in an inevitable non-equivalency, which one encounters, if one goes on reflecting until one reaches this level.[3] In what way this fundamental paradox constantly recurs under various aspects, all of them lying on a similar level, can be demonstrated by the two above-mentioned instances of contradiction among others.

If, at an ordinary level, that is lying within plurality, two opinions or standpoints clash, then a conciliation between them is somewhere possible. It appears that, to arrive at truth, one of them has to concede something, and the second something else, and in that case a union of the two standpoints, a theory without conflict is attained. If, however, one confronts the specifically human point of view—which thinks in the "pairs of opposites": the true (or untrue), the good (or evil), etc., one of which can be ascribed to everything—with the divine point of view, which is beyond all that, then it becomes obvious that, in the latter case, ascription *cannot* always take place, and no equivalency can be found. For the only thing man can say is: one thing *is better* than the other; we must see to it that the world achieves the better thing. For God, however, Who is perfect, also irrespective of the world and its conditions, it makes essentially no difference, whether the world is more or less good. Or, to put it in the words of the other "antinomy": all is equally near to Him. On the one hand this seems to be very unjust; on the other, however, it is sublime, the expression of highest grace. This is the non-equivalency expressed in the parable of the labourers in the vineyard.[4] Those who had worked since the morning, and those who had only done so during the eleventh hour, received the same wage.—Or, to put it all in different words: all that *man* can do is always to strive after the better, and ever to try to *approach* God. Within plurality, there exists indeed a difference between the better (to which all should be made to correspond) and the worse, and between a greater or smaller distance from God, and the better and the holier is *nearer* to God. God, however, conversely, is always equally near to every point of His creation. That is why He can also be "in the cheating of the cheat",[5] as well as at and behind many unimportant things. That is why there is grace and remission of sins. In that being-equally-near we have the non-equivalency, which seems to be unjust, if one looks upon it from plurality, from man, who is saying: am I not better, did I not do more than he? Within plurality things are weighed against each other; as for instance in the case of Karma. But beyond it that which is merely human equivalency comes to an end. Insofar as non-equivalency is essential and lasting here (within plurality it should always be removed), the "fundamental paradox" manifests itself as the highest or fundamental principle of creation.

Now it is also possible to stop arguing according to equivalency altogether and to endeavour to take from the outset the standpoint of the One Self or suprasubject, viewing the world therefrom. In that case one argues by means of essential non-equivalency. Hegelians do the same in their "dialectic method," which leaves behind the ordinary laws of logic. Says the late Professor Bolland in his *Zuivere Rede en hare Werkelijkheid* (Pure Reason and its Reality): "The true is this: to distinguish oneself in oneself; to posit the other from oneself; in order therein to come to oneself; to reverse it; and to be for oneself".[6] This can be related to that which was said above concerning God's perfection and man's struggle to approach Him. If we place ourselves in the position of the suprasubject (and as "we" are a unity of suprasubject and infrasubject, we are, as a matter of fact, always able to a certain extent to do so,[7] then it may be said, that this subject has made in itself the distinction between God and man, and has posited man as something else, opposite to itself. Man, however, strives after perfection and union with, approach to, God. Therein God comes to or realizes Himself. For it cannot be said, on the other hand, that man's perfection is totally and wholly indifferent to God: it may be true that He is always Himself and lastingly perfect, the world apart, but on the other hand the bringing into perfection of the different worlds, the approach of creatures cannot altogether be left out: He *can* do without, nevertheless He is more in these things than not. Sofar He is "for Himself": after man, from a more or less independent being, has once more become a fundamental part of God.

The antinomy and contradiction of perfection, contrasted with the struggle to be perfect, and those of the approach to God contrasted with His omnipresence, are solved in this way, if only one takes—across the gulf of non-equivalency—the all-embracing standpoint of deeper reasoning. In that case, the essence of all religion—the highest aspect of the world-in-plurality—*remains* the approach to God; on the other hand there is His grace, His coming near on every level, at every point. In the unity of these opposites creation is enacted; the drama of the universe is played through these opposites and their synthesis.

NOTES

[1] See *The Liberal Catholic*, Oct. 1936; *Variaties...*, p. 67 *seq.*

[2] Cp. *Tweeërlei Subjectiviteit*, p. 393.

[3] *Op. cit.*, §§ 24-25; 55-57.

[4] Matth. 20, 1-16.

[5] *Bhagavad Gītā*, 10, 36.

[6] On the title-page.

[7] Cp. *Tweeërlei Subjectiviteit*, p. 5; 519.

VI

OBJECTS AND OBJECT OF THE THEOSOPHICAL SOCIETY[1]

In "On the Watch-Tower" of the September *Theosophist* Dr. Arundale invites the expression of opinions on the changing of the Objects of The Theosophical Society.

In this connection the writer wishes to raise the following point: Should not there, really, be *only one aim or object* of the Theosophical movement, one idea underlying all the more specialized objects? Would it be possible to express this One Object in a few words? It may appear not to be practical to incorporate this idea in the Rules; nevertheless let us go into the matter for its own sake. Moreover, consideration of the One Object may throw light on the necessary alterations of the three Objects.

First, the writer would like to say that it seems to him that the new wording, proposed by Dr. Arundale, especially of the Second Object, is not yet quite satisfactory. The new version would include ". . a . . study of. . . the arts." Now a study of the arts means either Æsthetics or the History of Art. Agreed that both are fine subjects for study by Theosophists. But what about the *practice of art?* About the performing of music, about painting, sculpture and dancing themselves? An important difference exists between the study of, *i.e.*, the acquiring of knowledge about the arts—æsthetics and the history of art—and, though one sometimes speaks of "studying the piano," the practising or the cultivation of some art itself. Particularly when one is creatively engaged with some art, one can hardly call it a "study" of that art. The proposed wording of the Second Object does not sufficiently distinguish between the study about and the practice of some art, giving the impression that only the former is encouraged by Theosophy.

A second point is the clause, *a comparative study*, in the same Object. If The Theosophical Society decided to adopt this formulation, it would solve an old difficulty in a definite direction. The Society has, of course, a perfect right to do so, and it certainly is much better than the present state of ambiguity, but it should at least be done with full awareness of its signification. The old wording runs: "To encourage the study of comparative religion, philosophy and science". Now to us there is no doubt that those who designed this Object intended "comparative" to qualify "religion" only, and not "philosophy" or "science." "Comparative religion" forms an established notion indicating a part of Theology which is of special interest to Theosophists, as it proffers arguments for the unity of the religions. "Comparative science" is not an established notion; in philosophy the term is very rare as one usually distinguishes between the history of philosophy (which *might* be called "comparative philosophy") and systematic philosophy. Though there seems to be no doubt, therefore, as to how the ancient [existing] Second Object should be read, it is curious to note that at least two National Sections of The Society have understood "comparative" as qualifying all three nouns, and so the translation into the French language runs: *Encourager l'étude comparée des religions, de la philosophie et de la science;* and that into Dutch: *Het aanmoedigen van de vergelijkende studie van godsdienst, wijsbegeerte en wetenschap.* But the German Section—may it soon be revived—quite correctly translated "comparative religion" by *vergleichende Religionswissenschaft*, and its Second Object ran: *Zum Studium der vergleichenden Religionswissenschaft, der Philosophie und der Wissenschaften anzuregen.* In the writer's opinion this is the right translation; those of the French and Dutch Sections should simply be regarded as wrong.

If and when the Objects are reworded, attention should certainly be paid to this point, so that there can be no doubt as to what is meant, and so that no discrepancies can exist between the formulations of the various National Societies.

The Theosophical Society is, of course, perfectly free to choose the meaning of "comparative" that it thinks best. But if the wording "comparative study"—proposed on p. 504 of *On the Watch-Tower*—is adopted, similar objections as those to the "study of the arts" could in the writer's opinion be raised. Both formulae are too narrow. "Comparative study" is encouraged; *is creative study* then, *not* advocated? Should Theosophists refrain from creating something *new* in the sciences, in philosophy, in religion, art and so on, and if they do such a thing all the same, is that to be called non-Theosophical? Should they *restrict* themselves to comparing that which already exists?

This can hardly be meant, but all this points to the necessity of a broader definition of Theosophy. To take yet another example: is only the study of comparative religion to be encouraged, and not that of other parts of Theology, and not, which is still more important, the furthering of religion itself? The same remark applies here as was made with regard to the arts. The ancient Second Object was mainly conceived in view of the theoretical function of man, his intellectual study. Practice (apart from study itself being practice, as each thought is also an action) does not enter into the old Object, and the proposed rewording still speaks of the "study" of all that is mentioned. Now one would like to ask: is the furthering of religion, not the furthering of the study of it (which is Theology), but of its practice, Theosophical or not? The furthering, of course, of *any* religion is not Theosophical; but what about when Theosophists want to reform and rejuvenate a particular creed; what about when they want to start new forms of ritual and worship? Many Theosophists will be inclined to oppose such planning of religions-in-the-making, but, granted that The Theosophical Society as such should never be bound to any of them, can such work, successfully undertaken by a group of Theosophists, be called less Theosophical than small groups making a minute study of comparative religion?

We should hesitate to affirm that, and so again the necessity for a broader definition, offering at least scope for various kinds of activities, is emphasized. Some years ago the writer proposed such a definition,[2] and here part of what was written then will be repeated:

The world is a Unity including a Plurality, a Whole with its Parts. The Whole or God is always much more than the Parts, it transcends them; still it pervades them, it is immanent in them. The Unity is *always there* and yet there are degrees of Unity *within* the world or manifestation. (The contradiction of Unity always being there and at the same time but imperfectly, only more or less being there, is a "fundamental paradox"[3]). So within the world either Unity can be emphasized or Plurality (Diversity).

The *Theosophist*, according to us, is he who, being himself a unity or a centre within plurality, is aiming at Unity, or Synthesis or Harmony, or Integration, either with the Original Unity or God, or who is trying—in connection with that first attempt—to establish more Unity or Synthesis or Harmony or Integration within the world. Theosophy is, in short, a *synthetical* movement, a movement aiming at synthesis.

Others are *Pluralists*. They may resist unity or harmony by a destructive attitude in life, by emphasizing a certain part of the world, *e.g.*, by exclusively adhering to a restricted ideal like one historical creed or trend, or one particular nation or state. There are philosophers who do not consider the world to be a whole.

The Theosophist, however, strives after an all-embracing Unity. This Unity should be—as the word "synthesis" indicates—a Unity *in Diversity:* the parts must be there and retain as a rule their own character, but they should remain parts and not claim to be the whole.

From this definition of Theosophy as a synthetical movement both the existing Objects and the required additions can be inferred.

The pursuance of Unity falls into first, the striving of Man or the individual after union *with God* in the three following forms, according to the three faculties of consciousness: reflection on God and finally contemplation of God, or, seen from the exterior, Religious Philosophy or Theology; personal surrender and devotion to God, or Mysticism; and gradual actual union with God, or Yoga. Secondly, man, inspired by that divine unity, turns *to the world*, and tries to establish unity within it; whence other cultural values arise. When he tries to understand the world or plurality, then Science and Philosophy come into existence. When he strives after a practical unity between existing parts of plurality, his aim is Love and Brotherhood: harmony between kingdoms of nature, creeds, races, nations, classes and sexes. When he tries to create certain separate unities within the world, though reflecting the whole, Art and (*e.g.*, ceremonial) Magic are the result.

This definition includes the old Objects, which seem to emphasize certain aspects that played a part in the history of the Theosophical movement. But it also includes the study of all true philosophy and science in themselves, comparative or creative; and also the practice of art, the making of religion, insofar as useful and noble (related to the whole!); yoga and mysticism (which are not mentioned in the old three Objects!).

Ought one to fear that this definition is too broad? In what, then, lies the difference between the ordinary scientist, artist, and so on, and the Theosophist? The difference is that, according to this ideal, the whole is always kept in view. So Theosophy admonishes the scientist to pay more heed to the whole and to the background of life than to its many details; the artist to express the divine unity of things, instead of reflecting cleverly ugly parts. Moreover, the Theosophist wants to establish *unity between the various cultural values*. The latter have, of course, their own uniqueness or autonomy, but nevertheless science and religion, art and morality, science and brotherhood, should not clash, but unite in their efforts. It is obvious that the desirability of some other activities of Theosophists, such as pacifism (within certain limits) and vegetarianism also emanate from this definition of Theosophy.

It will probably prove to be too radical to change the Objects of The Theosophical Society so that they meet the writer's definition, especially in these times. (And, by the way, is not much time and energy wasted in discussing and formulating juridical clauses?) But one might make the following slight changes, so that it runs:

"Being a *synthetical* movement, the One Object of The Theosophical Society is the furthering of *Unity* in Diversity, which aim implies more particularly the following three declared Objects:

First: To form a nucleus of the Universal Brotherhood of Life without distinction of kingdom-of-nature, race, creed, sex, caste or colour.

Second: To encourage the study of Philosophy, Religion, Science and Civic Conditions, and particularly of Comparative Religion, and of the unrecognized laws of nature and the hidden powers of man.

Third: To promote the right practice of Religion, Art and Politics.

In these ways the old Second and Third Objects are combined as they both refer to study or investigation. On the other hand the whole aspect of practice is united in a new Third Object. The clause "more particularly" at the beginning of the writer's proposed version admits of other objects than the three mentioned following from the One Object. So nothing is excluded, as was the case in the old Objects. Thus a broader definition is given, while the time-honoured old Objects are maintained, and only a few necessary new provisions are added.[4]

NOTES

[1] See *The Theosophist*, LXI, 5, Febr. 1940, p. 461 *seq.* and *Variaties...*, p. 205 *seq.*

[2] "A Broader Definition of Theosophy", *Theos. World-University Quarterly Bulletin* 1932, p. 25 *seq.*; "Een ruimere definitie van Theosofie", *De Theosofische Beweging*, May 1932, p. 199 *seq.*; *De Pionier* II, p. 354 *seq.*; "Eine neue Wesensbestimmung der Theosophie", *Theosophische Studien*, IV, p. 57 *seq.*

[3] Cp. *Tweeërlei Subjectiviteit*, p. 394 *seq.*

[4] Since the above was written, the texts of the Second Object underwent some changes in various European National Sections, but not always for the better.

VII

THE FUNDAMENTAL PARADOX[1]

In philosophy an ancient tradition can be observed, *viz.*, to establish a *highest*, a basic principle. If the individual sciences have already succeeded in grouping ever greater units of knowing under one viewpoint, how much more beautiful it would be to summarize the whole of reality from one point of view. However, as all of you know, the results of these efforts cannot be called felicitous, but rather, if not exactly naïve, then at least very often one-sided. Discouraged on that account, many philosophers have abandoned the quest for a highest principle. In any case it might be said that such a principle should meet certain very special requirements. For example, it should be related to Being as well as to Thinking, it would have to be a *principium essendi*[2] as well as a *principium cognoscendi*.[3] In it Being and Thinking should be interrelated. So the difficulties to be overcome before a satisfactory formula is achieved are not inconsiderable. This fact, however, does not seem to me to be a valid reason for giving up every attempt to establish it. It is the same with systematics: nowadays little is heard in favour of it. Neither does the unsatisfactory nature of the systems devised so far constitute a good reason for abandoning all endeavours to establish an all-round tenable system of thought. It only means that the systems hitherto designed are not at the same time sufficiently broad, deep and clear-cut. Now in a tenable system the problem of a highest or central principle should also be solved.

All this is a matter of *metaphysics*. Is metaphysics, then, possible as a science? Is metaphysics still actual? With regard to the question as to the sense of metaphysics, in any case two definitions should be distinguished. Firstly, philosophers such as Fechner, Wundt and Heymans have during the last hundred years framed a notion of metaphysics in a narrower sense, based on experience: *auf Grundlage der Erfahrung.*[4] What they had in mind amounts to a discussion of the relationship between spirit and matter, or rather between consciousness and the body, to a confrontation of the results of psychology with those of the natural sciences. Whether one is inclined to call this metaphysics or not, it is certain that, as an aim, it has sense. There is, however, yet another definition of "metaphysics" which is more in accordance with tradition. In this connection the simplest course is to call metaphysics the doctrine of the Absolute. It is against this definition of metaphysics that the usual scepticism regarding metaphysics as a science creeps in. And yet, if philosophy is ever to succeed in summing up the whole of reality from one point of view, and to succeed in establishing a highest or central principle, then an access should be found to this supposed centre of all, to something that is absolute as contrasted with the relativity of multiple things.

There are plenty of philosophers who point out to us such an access, but their point of departure far from convinces every one. It reminds one too much of what can be observed in dogmatic theology: given a certain starting-point reasoning is keen enough, but what is lacking is belief in that starting-point. Sometimes it seems as if a certain mystical experience were needed to grasp the starting-point of metaphysics, an experience which is not given to every one. If this happened to be the last word that could be said in this connection, thinking people would divide themselves into two camps: those who are able to achieve this central vision, and those for whom this vision is permanently elusive. Now it may be true that in philosophy every individual has ultimately to realize arguments for himself, and demonstrations visible to a multitude of persons are impossible; nevertheless it is advisable not to be satisfied with a mystical experience that is only accessible to certain types of men as the basis of metaphysics. It may be true that there are people to whom any reasoning or calculation that is not very simple cannot be made clear. But disregarding the latter, a satisfactory starting point for metaphysics should be such that it can be made evident without too much difficulty to a great number of men, merely by drawing their attention to certain facets of the problem concerned.

Let me give an example to make clear what I have in mind. There is a contemporary French philosopher, LOUIS LAVELLE (1883-1951), who is called an existentialist. In my opinion he is either no existentialist or existentialism is different from and far deeper than that for which it is generally taken. For Lavelle the point of departure in metaphysics is *l'être pur*, pure Being, and that is realized in an *expérience initiale ou parfaite.*[5] I am among the first to acknowledge that important conclusions can be inferred from that, which, if they do not directly tally with those at which I arrive, run strikingly parallel to them. But is not the situation with Lavelle's basic experience like this: whosoever realizes it in the same way, can follow him: but for those who are not able to do so his conclusions remain a closed book? What I miss here is the coercing element. If one is, in fact, to start from an experience or realization, then this experience should be more closely circumscribed, or rather localized: one should be placed face to face with it.

In this connection I might add the following general remark. If metaphysics in the lower and more simple sense is based *auf Grundlage der Erfahrung*, it does not follow that metaphysics in the deeper and more important sense should *not* be based on experience. For all those fundamental principles of the various philosophical systems often amount to mere reasonings which have little to do with reality. Conversely, however, if it should be possible to introduce also on this level a factor of experience, it would have great weight. Reasoning can follow, provided that experience precedes it. So Lavelle is, in my opinion, quite right in starting from an experience; but the nature of Lavelle's experience is to me too vague.

I now want to remind you of the fact that some philosophers thought that they had discovered a difficulty or *aporia* in the I. HEINRICH RICKERT, for instance, writes in his *Der Gegenstand der Erkenntnis* [6] about the difficulty of objectifying the subject. We know of ourselves, but that means that we are the knowing I and the known I at the same time, which, according to Rickert, involves a contradiction. HERBART writes in the same vein. Rickert quotes Schopenhauer who in this connection talks of the *Weltknoten*, the knot of the world, and of the limit of all philosophy.[7] Rickert, however, denies that one should encounter here the identity of the knowing and the known. If that were the case, he says, then one would, in fact, have here the insoluble knot of the world, the eternal paradox. He rejects the assumption that it should be so. Both he and Herbart look for a way out of the difficulty by putting one part of the I opposite the other part, for instance, that which was felt yesterday as contrasted with the I that knows today. But I cannot accept this way out. We are certainly able today to survey and to judge our moods of yesterday. But that is not the point. The point is that the I knows of its existence here and now at one and the same instant. How is that possible? How is it possible for the complete I to know itself, and *be* at the same moment? One should not try to evade the difficulty involved in self-consciousness as Rickert and Herbart attempt to do. One should have the courage to look into the eyes of Medusa. If one encounters here an eternal paradox, this paradox should be established and acknowledged. In any case, this is likely to prove a remarkable situation.

Now we shall try to reach the root of the problem as far as possible. Therefore I propose that you perform the following thought-experiment, and observe what happens: "I think that I think that I think, etc." This is an effort of the will to objectify the subject. The latter never completely succeeds, since the knowing subject is ever again present as the subject of the new effort of knowing. The subject continues to escape the attempt to turn it into an object. Though one renews the effort, one constantly retains but an empty shell. Nevertheless we *know* of the subject; it is even regularly quoted as a paragon of certainty as when one says "as true as I am". The certainty of this is a criterion for certainties of another kind. Nevertheless the usual requirement that the mind should be able to objectify in itself the object that is to be known can never be met. Notwithstanding that there is certainty here, paradigmatic certainty. Therefore there is here the primordial identity of the knower and the known. In that there lies a contradiction, or rather an eternal paradox, a world-knot that cannot be avoided, but which we have to recognize. As the whole situation seems to be so central, I am inclined to speak of it as *the fundamental paradox (le paradoxe fondamental, das Grundparadoxon)*.

This might also appear to be the way in which the highest principle for which we are looking can be found. In any case, the requirement that both Being and Thinking should be involved, that they should be interrelated here, is met. Another important feature is that the factor of experience is not lacking. It should be noted that, if one goes on to reflect upon the *contents* of this fundamental paradox, at least the starting-point was empirical—we have even wilfully made use of a thought-experiment. As a starting-point this experiment is far more exact, far more closely circumscribed than is, in general, *une expérience initiale de l'être pur*. It looks as if, among all our experiences, we have ascended to this very point, being the highest within experience. The highest principle, then, could be established through the highest experience. If one starts reflecting, on the other hand, upon the notion of it, then the highest principle can become a central or basic principle, from which, if nothing interferes, one should be able to deduce the whole of reality.

In order to know more about the notion of this paradox, in order to investigate whether a central or basic principle can be obtained in this way, we shall have to return to the thought-experiment which we have already carried out. We have observed that the subject in its entirety and reality for ever escapes or eludes efforts to objectify it: we were left with a mere empty shell; the subject itself was ever again present as the subject of the new act or effort of knowing. It eludes one for ever, and nevertheless it is real—a paragon of reality. Now that which continually escapes, and nevertheless is real, is nothing but the Absolute, which is that which is essentially released (cp. *absolvo*). It should be stated here that the Absolute is encountered in pure self-consciousness, and can be experienced, experimentally realized by every one, if only one's attention is drawn to the situation. That the Absolute, however, should be involved in the highest or central principle is another requirement that we have made. Beside this, or beneath this, there is the effort of knowing as the prototype of all endeavours generally to bring into relationship, and so of the Relative and of the Multiple. We also have here Being as against Knowing. So, after all, there is reason in speaking of a *fundamental* paradox.

Now can the notion of this paradox be more closely circumscribed or formulated? We shall certainly have to try this, but it can be expected that the intrinsic difficulty of making an object of the subject will return. For, if we try to determine the relationship between the pure subject as that which for ever escapes and is therefore the Absolute, and the remainder of being, what one gets is the relationship between that which is essentially without relation, or the Relationless, and "Relation in general". But one cannot properly speak of a *relationship* between the Relationless and Relation-in-general, unless as a very special kind of relationship that is really no relationship. As a relationship it is, in contrast to all other relations, a very special, a one-sided relationship: this relation so to speak gazes upward towards the Relationless, but never reaches it. On the other hand, from on high, from the Relationless, there is no proper connection with Relation-in-general.

This can also be expressed thus: that the Relationless behaves as if it were indifferent whether the other is there or not, for it remains for ever relationless or absolute in itself. It is as if the one term of the relationship which is the fundamental paradox wholly includes or embraces the other term, or as if the second is *as nothing* when compared with the first. And yet the second term is something, though a tiny something, for we become aware of the Relationless just because it continually repels or denies the other term. As that which is repelled or denied it is at least *something*. And yet the second term is, as a fact, wholly cancelled out by the first, this being the Absolute or that which is essentially released. So the second is nothing and at the same time something. This is no inexact formulation, but, on the contrary, in this very contradiction the fundamental paradox again comes forth. One should bear in mind that all this is no playing with words, but an endeavour to render the notion of the relationship between, on the one hand, the subject which our thought in vain tries to objectify and, on the other hand, our thought, whilst one knows all the time that this subject is an example of certainty. It can be said that real knowledge for which the first condition is that the subject has something before itself in the act of knowing and which, in that case, is known adequately, is never possible here. One might call the knowledge that yet is all the time present in this case (since the I as an example of certainty is even known before all other things) a knowledge nevertheless, a *knowledge quand même*. Likewise the notion of the fundamental paradox itself can only be known or worded *quand même*. That is why one always becomes entangled in images while attempting to define it.

Still a little more can be said concerning the contents of the fundamental paradox. The first term of it is in proportion to the second as the principle of the Same *(das Selbe, tauton)* to that of the Other *(das Andere, thateron)*. Thinking in general is typical of plurality, thinking that tries to coerce the subject in the relation of, firstly, an idea, secondly, of the subject, corresponding, thirdly, with the object concerned (which is in this case the subject itself: this is why the effort always fails). On the other hand, of the subject one but knows that it remains for ever identical with itself. This subject is always the same, and therefore Identity in principle. Opposite to this there is the effort of knowing as Plurality in principle, or, compared with Identity in principle, the Other *(das Andere)*, or Difference in principle. These principles of the Same and the Other, *tauton* and *thateron*, become or are united in the fundamental paradox in such a way that the Other is as nothing as against the Same; the second term, as we have seen, is cancelled out by the first. If one, however, does not consider the unity of the Same and the Other in the paradox, but if one picks them out as independent principles, then one can maintain that the whole further world springs from their contrast. From the Other, or from Difference in principle, all minor differences, the whole of plurality, proceed, while the Same as the original unity remains for ever opposed to and above plurality. In my book *Tweeërlei Subjectiviteit* (Twofold Subjectivity) I deal with this deduction of the entire further plurality, in detail. I endeavour, for instance, to prove that the antithesis of the Same and the Other is converted into the contrast between respectively the Real (or the Hylic, *das Hylische*) and the Ideal (or the Eidetic, *das Eidetische*). Plurality, namely, acts upon the substratum of the Same and then the Real comes into being, split up into the many empirical points or subjects; unity, on the other hand, acts upon the substratum of the Other and so the whole or the realm *(das Reich)* of the Ideal, of ideas and values, arises. At this juncture the centre of gravity is shifted: while the Same carries far more weight than the Other, the Ideal is, on the contrary, the task *(die Aufgabe)* for the Real. But I cannot hope to convince you as to all these details within the scope of this address. So I would refer you to my book.

I shall only go into a few more points. It can be said that *equivalence* is characteristic of plurality. In plurality one term is either equivalent to the other, or a tendency can continually be noticed towards establishing the equal, towards counterbalancing things by way of compensation. It is not without reason that the statement A=A, or A=non-non-A, constitutes the simplest formula of logic. Likewise equivalence plays an important part elsewhere, *e.g.*, in the laws of conservation in the sciences. Against all this it can be pointed out that the fundamental paradox is essentially non-equivalent. The pure subject can never be adequately known, so that it is out of the question that one should be able to state here: now *this* is equal to *that*. So it is not a case of contradiction in the lower sense which should be eliminated, after which equivalence is re-established, but, as Rickert also pointed out, there exists in connection with the subject which tries to know itself a really inevitable contradiction. If one realizes that this contradiction cannot be evaded, because the subject, as a fact, completely but inadequately knows itself here and now, then one has established experimentally an insoluble contradiction, an everlasting non-equivalence, in other words, what we have called the fundamental paradox. Then one should proceed to show that wherever others also speak of inevitable contradictions—as Hegel does—there is question, in so far as they are tenable, of the same basic paradox.

This non-equivalence is one of what I am inclined to call *moments* or aspects of the fundamental paradox. There are more of them. I refer to the moment of swinging or *oscillation*. If it can be said that the second term of the fundamental paradox is "nothing and yet something" as against the first, then the conception oscillates between that "something" and "nothing". That again is here unavoidable. Conversely, this aspect of oscillation will be found everywhere where the basic paradox manifests itself.

Plurality divides itself into various subordinate fields or respects *(Hinsichten)*, such as those of Thinking or thought, of Being (multiple being), of Happening, of Time and so on. Now in all these respects the fundamental paradox with its various aspects or moments will recur. Regarded from a specific field or respect the Absolute assumes on every occasion a different form with its own *aporias* or difficulties of understanding. I try to show that in all those cases the difficulty can be reduced to one and the same fundamental paradox, and that its aspects such as non-equivalence, oscillation and others also recur. As *aporias*, as difficulties of this kind, I mention, for example, that of the Self-caused Cause, the *causa sui* or the prime mover; that of the Eternal Now; that which is situated between the notions of One and Two, or that of the Limit; and others. Likewise, that in connection with the pure subject or I—from which we started—is among them. Time again prevents my entering into these applications of the notion of the basic paradox as I have done in my book on the subject.

However, for one application of the fundamental paradox I would make an exception. I am thinking of its application to the *concept of God.* If the philosophy of religion contrasts the transcendence with the immanence of God, difficulties have always been met with these notions. For, on the one hand, God, if He is God and absolute, must of necessity be wholly transcendent: must exist in Himself quite apart from the question whether there is a world or not. In this way one arrives at the ancient problem: why was it necessary for God to create the world? And God, on the other hand, should nevertheless always be conceived as working in the world, as immanent. After all, the world and the realization of values in it belong to God, and He is more after His passing through the world than before. Whereas transcendence obviously represents the deepest viewpoint, embracing or cancelling out the other, that other, the immanence, is indeed as *nothing* compared with transcendence, and yet it is continually *some*thing. Such oscillation cannot be avoided here. It is the same oscillation one encounters in the fundamental paradox. Equivalence is also lacking here. This might be put in the following way. The whole of religion propagates the approach to God: "Nearer, my God, to Thee."[8] On the other hand it must be true that God is equally near to every point of His creation. Is the approach to Him, then, not superfluous? These reflections have been partly voiced in the parable of the labourers in the vineyard.[9] Those who had worked since the morning, and those who had only done so during the last hour of the day, received the same wages. The first group of labourers grumbled because of the lack of equivalence, which here too, is held to be the law of the world. But the grace of God is non-equivalent. Thus the concept of the basic paradox throws light on the concept of God.

At this juncture it should be noted that, if I say that the Absolute can be experienced in self-consciousness, if only the attention is drawn to it, then it should be added that that pure I which can never be objectified, though it is a paragon of certainty, is no longer the empirical subject, Mr. A or Miss B each having such and such a character, etc. No, the pure subject, the deepest self, experienced by one person cannot be distinguished from the pure subject, the deepest self, experienced by another person. Therefore they coincide, and there exists but One pure subject, which I call the *suprasubject.* The sharp contrast between the One pure I or suprasubject and the many "infrasubjects," fallible, mortal, differing from each other, is the main theme of my book on "Twofold Subjectivity" already mentioned. I can again only allude to the consequences which the sharp distinction of this twofold subjectivity brings about in regard to the Kantian problems, *e.g.*, in regard to the objectivity of our knowledge after the application of the apriori to the dates of experience. In my opinion the objectivity of our knowledge can only be established, if the apriori is indeed psychologically existent in the minds of the infrasubjects, but originates in the One suprasubject, which, on the one hand, has brought forth the world and its deepest laws within itself, and which, on the other hand, has planted an apriori knowledge concerning these laws in the infrasubjects. In this case the infrasubject possesses some knowledge about the general features of the world which is valid independently from himself, the infrasubject. Then *realism* can be reconciled with *idealism*: at the level of the infrasubject properties can belong to things, while nevertheless the whole of plurality is ultimately the immanent idea of the One suprasubject.

But we are digressing from the fundamental paradox. What is the use, I would ask, of reducing everything to a principle that can never be completely thought out? Let me point out that, immediately below the basic paradox, equivalence (A=A) reigns, and here everything *can* be rationalized. Generally speaking we encounter here the problem of the *Irrational.* Now I feel inclined to distinguish sharply between what I call the *infra*rational and the *supra*rational. All the problems that have not yet been solved, but which can be solved in principle, are infrarational. Many of this kind exist, and one should not jump to the conclusion that one has to do with something that is permanently irrational. Apart from that, however, there is one respect in which a complete rationalization or "equalizing", saying: A is B or is C, is not feasible. That is in respect to the basic paradox which can be demonstrated in the effort to make an object of the pure I or subject. Here, at the roots of thinking, we are at the level of the suprarational, and this suprarationality of the fundamental paradox is the core of all the talk about the irrational. One should, however, be very cautious in deciding where reduction to the basic paradox is permissible and indicated, and where not. In principle reduction is only permissible in that one respect. Only at the pure I or the suprasubject is the fundamental paradox real, and can it be experienced. In so far, however, as the paradox is observed from certain specific fields, it recurs in them, and it appears there in a slightly modified form. In so far as God coincides with the one pure I or suprasubject—only, of course, with the *one*, *pure* I—the contents of the basic paradox obtained at the pure I with its typical difficulties also return in the concept of God. Similarly, one has conceived the notion of a *causa sui* or prime mover, since the need was felt to break the endless chain—with its equivalence—of causes and effects. It is the same with the Eternal Now, or with the One as the original unity, the foundation of all numbers. The same Absolute recurs in all these instances in various forms, but accompanied by the same difficulty of elucidation. There is but one Absolute; there can be no question of a series of them. Likewise it can be said that there is merely *one* miracle or mystery; there is no place for many. In the meantime, it would seem to me very useful if many mysteries could be reduced to one. If it could be shown that the same principle that can never be wholly elucidated, with the same aspects of non-equivalence, oscillation, etc., recurs in many cases, then much would be gained, then we should have but one instead of many difficulties. If it further appears that this one aporia is insolvable, since the roots, the limits of thoughts—thought, which always thinks in terms of plurality—are reached, then one could decide to what extent the irrational makes sense. There is sense in the irrational at the fundamental paradox which is suprarational. There, no ordinary rational knowledge is possible, at most a knowledge *quand même*, "nevertheless". Apart from this there is no sense in the irrational; apart from this the irrational is infrarational, and it should—in the field of thought—be replaced by the rational as soon as possible. By localizing in the fundamental paradox, however, that of the irrational which is tenable, the path is cleared for the normal process of rationalization.

Finally I would point out that, if what I have suggested in regard to the basic paradox is right, this does not concern a new principle. It must always have been valid; only the name is new, and part of the formulation. I have no time to quote a number of philosophers to whom the same or a similar thought has occurred. Let me cite but one. If SCHELLING[10] says that the Absolute is not only the unity of the opposites, but the unity of the unity and of the opposites, then that is the fundamental paradox, since the second term of it is continually nothing or embraced by the first, the former remaining nevertheless identical with itself. Therein lies the paradox.

NOTES

[1] Address delivered at Amsterdam, August 12th, 1948, at the Tenth International Congress of Philosophy. See *Proceedings*, p. 407 *seq.*; *The Theosophist*, LXX; *De Grondparadox*, p. 9 *seq.*

[2] Principle of Being.

[3] Principle of Knowing.

[4] On the basis of experience.

[5] Initial or perfect experience.

[6] *The Object of Cognition* (3d. ed., p. 43 *seq.*).

[7] *Werke*, (Frauenstädt), Vol. I, p. 143.

[8] Cp. *supra*, Ch. V.

[9] Matth. 20, 1-16.

[10] In: Bruno, *Werke* IV, p. 236.

VIII

THE WORLD-TEACHER AND CONTRADICTIONS

(The Order of the Star in the East, founded in 1911 and led by prominent Theosophists, had announced the coming of a great teacher, a World-Teacher, though not necessarily a return of the Christ. At a series of gatherings, especially at the large gatherings (of 2000-3000 people) during the Starcamps at Ommen in the Netherlands, expectations ran high. Several times the World-Teacher was believed to have spoken through the mouth of J. Krishnamurti. However, a crisis developed: Krishnamurti's teachings took a different turn from that which has been expected of him by theosophists. Besides, the Order of the Star in the East was dissolved by him.)

The Star-camp at Ommen of 1929 has for some time now been a thing of the past, and it may at present be the right thing to devote some considerations to it. It would be hardly any use to deny that KRISHNAJI's teachings have found different echoes: different as regards the feelings evoked, which go from the purest enthusiasm to surprise or even to a kind of indignation; and different as regards the conclusions drawn and the decisions arrived at. Undoubtedly confusion has arisen and a parting of the ways set in: for many it has meant uncertainty, incomprehension; for others the taking of opposite directions without hesitation. Everything that, with this given state of affairs, can contribute towards elucidation or merely to reflection should be welcomed. No attempt to deceive ourselves or outsiders with respect to the existing difficulties should be allowed to taint a movement like ours. Whoever wants to arrive at a reconciliation of the discrepancies will have to do so wittingly and after mature consideration.

If animated by these intentions, one tries to account for the development of things one perceives in the first place that the lines that had been drawn in the past year or even previous to that—at Ommen as well as at Ojai—have been lengthened; that there has been no question of mitigating or making conspicuous the other side of the picture, but that, contrary to the expectation of many, everything has been expressed as consciously and intentionally as possible, quite straightforwardly, without any possibility of subterfuge or compromise.

Owing to this many of use have been faced with great difficulties.

For even when we continue to acknowledge Krishnaji as a great and important Teacher, even while wishing him every success, this is not yet sufficient. If we are to listen to his teachings wholeheartedly; if we are to agree personally with the World-Teacher, now that he seems to be there, it is necessary for us that we should be able to rhyme his utterances with things that we think we know for certain from other sources; or else we have to put the latter aside as being false. Take for instance the communications from the Star-camp of 1925 about the indication of several disciples, about the importance of certain movements, like the one for Theosophical Education and a Theosophical University and the one for the Liberal Catholic Church—also and especially in connection with the advent of the World-Teacher. About all this nothing more is heard. Quite the contrary; about Theosophy hardly anything at all is said, let alone about a special activity; on ceremonies, nay on all religious bodies censure is passed. And about the purposiveness and intention of this there is no further possibility of doubt.

The solution we offered, after the previous camp-congress at Ommen, in the November-number 1928 of the Dutch periodical *Theosophia*, is no longer acceptable either. Under the heading "Secundary or Primary" we then suggested that the meaning of Krishnaji's utterances was that we should somewhere lay a *stress* that is only too often forgotten. Indeed, we wrote, all these societies and movements, all ceremonies and intellectual distinctions are only of secondary importance, and although in this respect our movements have spoken a better language than others (was the independence of the disciple not already a Theosophical doctrine? When did the Liberal Catholic Church ever advocate—as is usually done elsewhere—obligatory participation in, sole salvation through the Sacraments?), yet it is absolutely necessary for all of us to be reminded of the primary importance of the One, all forms embracing Life. Here we have all of us still much to learn, and the putting in the foreground of such a fundamental principle, even while passing over other important matters, is the very thing we should have expected from a World-Teacher. Apart from that *we* can go quietly on devoting ourselves partly to those other matters, for, the moment we fix our gaze on the Plurality of phenomena instead of seeing everything only from the viewpoint of the deepest Unity—and this is bound to happen alternately—,we shall feel that it is of permanent importance to go on combating and working for the Good, the True, the Beautiful and the Holy *within* that Plurality.[1] —And in a study on life and form Bishop Arundale had come to a similar result in *The Watchtower* of September 1928: "So I hold these forms ever so lightly, though I honour them and treat them with the reverence which is their due." [2]

The remarkable thing is that such a standpoint, such a way out of the difficulties no longer appears possible. For Krishnaji has expressly repeated his rejection of all forms, especially in connection with religious purposes, including not only ceremonies, but also all organisations with a religious object, without distinguishing between new and old, liberal or orthodox. In consequence of which the number for instance of those who turn their backs on the Liberal Catholic Church, the spoiled child of 1925, has increased and the Theosophical Society also counts apostates. And so we have now a growing unrest and a parting of the ways has begun. A group can be pointed out of those who want to stick to Krishnaji through thick and thin; who are prepared to give up everything for his sake, also the work of years (and if necessary to leave it to destruction), hoping sincerely in this way to attain Liberation. Then there are those who doubt and hesitate and do not see their way. Others are engaged in endeavours (not very successfull so far in our opinion) to combine the one with the other. Finally there are those who are deeply convinced that their work amidst forms is so important (although on a secondary level), so helpful to others and to the world, so beautiful in itself, that they have to go on with it,even if it should bring them into conflict with Krishnaji, whom they also take to be the World-Teacher. As someone said to me: "As it is Krishnaji's vocation to be World-Teacher, so it is mine to be a priest of the L.C.C.". Moreover these people maintain that the Presence of Christ in the Sacraments is for them beyond any doubt, a matter of personal experience; the reality of "Christ without" *cannot* be altogether denied.[3] Be it as it may, in a wider sense we are all confronted by the following question: Let it be granted, that the Teacher had to bring something new that could not be foreseen, and that it could not be expected that he would give a kind of course of Theosophical lectures—; were then those people, was Annie Besant, who has indicated Krishnaji as the future Teacher, and prepared the way for him, *right* in that indication (and in her announcement in 1925 of his near manifestation), but *mistaken* in her other messages from her Master? Ought perhaps the whole Order of the Star in the East, which in turn was an organisation with a spiritual purpose and a declaration of principles, not to have been founded?

As will been seen, we are confronted by difficulties in plenty and it seems to be worth while to go into them as deeply as possible. In doing so we shall take a road that has not yet been trodden in the meditations on the subject.[4]

What is the common supposition of all those, who have been plunged in uncertainty? The *principium contradictionis*: the principle that there exists finally but One Truth and that the relative truths, through which we try to express that One Truth, must not contradict each other; otherwise one of two theses must each time be erroneous. In other words, it cannot be *at the same time* true that the World-Teacher rejects apostles altogether and yet indirectly indicated them himself at a certain time; nor can he at the same time attach importance to ceremonies and consider them to be of no moment. Now the general tendency will be to solve a contradiction in this way, that one thesis is true all the same in one respect, and the other also, but in another, wider sense. In the case under consideration however all that would be tantamount to hairsplitting: after what has been said in this year, only one thing can, in our opinion, be maintained: that Krishnaji's meaning is now evident. Consequently there *are* contradictions. What are we to do with them?

The may-be-unexpected viewpoint we should like to suggest here is the following. This law, that no contradictions can be acknowledged to exist, refers especially to *Plurality*, to the manifested world. As we have expounded more extensively elsewhere,[5] man always thinks in terms of Plurality (*viz.* of subject and object and the relation between them) and about Plurality (about a plurality of moments). When, rising above Plurality or the manifested world to the original Unity or the unmanifested, we try to embody this viewpoint in the forms of our thinking, this will never be an entire success. We shall then always meet with contradictions or, as we have put it, the outcome will always be a "fundamental paradox", but never an ordinary, "equivalent", that is logical truth.—This assertion is in itself not so particularly new. Kant has among other things written about "antinomies", which are found if one goes deep enough in several directions, and the School of Hegel makes it its business to find out such fundamental uncertainties.

Perhaps the contradictions that have come to light in connection with the Order of the Star, ought to be seen in precisely such a philosophic light. And the difficulties might partly be caused by an inability to feel at home in the "dialectic" way of looking at things that is requisite here; by the usual demand: *either* the one *or* the other. It goes without saying that one has to be cautious with these dialectics. More or less profoundly differing in this from the School of Hegel, we feel inclined to emphasize that the usual laws of thinking and logic apply to Plurality and that, when dealing with plurality, we have to stick to them. Otherwise the door is opened for scepticism in the theoretical and for constant uncertainty in the practical domain. But as soon as there is a question of penetrating to these depths, we shall always encounter a similar contradiction or "fundamental paradox". Only, have we cause for speaking of such a fundamental contradiction in connection with Krishnaji's teachings? Not for instance if the World-Teacher is spoken of in connection with the apostles. This is so much a concrete question, one referring to plurality, that only one truth concerning it is possible. But there *is* cause for speaking of a fundamental paradox, when it comes to transcendental viewpoints or viewpoints having to do with the relation of the manifested world and the unmanifested. And now in this connection we are struck by the fact that a question which of late years has appeared most interesting of all: the anti-thesis of *Life* (the One Life, the Self etc.) and *Form* (*e.g.* ceremonies and organisations) is concerned with this very relation, bears precisely on the unmanifested versus the manifested world. There consequently we must expect to meet typical contradictions.

In what shape do they show themselves in this case? In that of a different, contradictory valuation: first a certain importance attached to ceremonies (1925) and later a strong rejection of such things. In this connection it will be well to distinguish between *valuation*, that is practically adopting and propagating a certain attitude towards things and a complete *theoretical* consideration of all viewpoints concerned. Taking the latter first: in our humble opinion the formula we proposed a year ago, which was assented to by several people, still contains the most obvious theoretical epitome: that on the one hand it goes without saying that Life is of primary importance, and on the other hand all forms are also of some moment, but only secondary. Which means that it is our duty (a duty in the performance of which we continually fail) to acknowledge the primary importance of the One Life, in comparison with which all the rest is as nothing, is entirely indifferent, but that on the other hand, in so far as we also permanently live in a world of form, we may, we must, on a secondary plane, work among forms, preferring those that are better, truer, more beautiful, holier or more divine. Although seen from the deepest viewpoint, all differences in the manifested world are unimportant, yet we must never relax our endeavours to realize *within* this world that which is better; nay, such is our imperative and sacred task. In this unimportance *plus* importance of forms lies such a fundamental and insoluble paradox as we have referred to above.

Whoever might have expected the Teacher to state, to express this necessary contradiction, this "as well. . . as. . .", has been disappointed. *He* does not want to be a philosopher; he does not go in for philosophizing. He appears on the other hand to consider it in the very first place his mission to get mankind to adopt *a changed attitude towards life*. For that purpose it is no use to form a theory that does justice to all viewpoints and throws light on all aspects; but to *propagate* one definite viewpoint, the deepest, the best, with all the theoretical onesidedness inherent to propaganda. Out of the antinomy of Life and Form, which have both in a sense justification, the Teacher chooses the deepest viewpoint [6] without hesitation, without considering the to-a-certain-extent-justified opposite conception. Such is his message from the Father: [7] from the deepest fundament of Universe and Nature. Certainly, as long as there is question of a manifested world, there will be form, but that is not his business: he has come to lay stress on Life, on the Unifying Principle, on Unity. In so far as he is the great Teacher, he is bound to be onesided, to bring us only that which is deepest of all; he wants no reflection, no weighing, but only doing, acting, choosing.

Looking at the present difficulties in this way: that the World-Teacher is necessarily onesided, because he wants, before everything else, to set an example, through a way of life, and not to construct an intellectual theory, we may find that much becomes understandable. For, in the first place, we need not in this case concern ourselves much about intellectual contradictions. In so far as *we* want to theorize all the same, we may then, in a certain measure, also attach importance to the other element. We—at least most of us—have not such an absolute mission entrusted to us and therefore we may also consider the other viewpoint, provided that we never forget that all forms have but secondary importance and that we always keep that restriction in mind—, and in the second place we may also strive to perfect those forms, nay, it is our duty to do so. *There lies the task that is left to us*. Some will feel the call more, others less, but it is a task that has to be performed—for within plurality one thing *is* better than another—and here marking time means retrogression. The very rejection of forms is a form, a choosing something at the cost of something else. It is, however, impossible to remain for ever at this height, where one understands that the highest form is in the formless, and where the individual experiences that he is absolutely free and finds Liberation. Granted that this experience cannot in its essence be brought down to a lower level without loosing that essence, yet all this has also to penetrate other things; the impulse imparted by the Teacher on such a high plane has to recreate that which lies lower and nearer the periphery. This ideal of a community, a state, a church, an education and so on directed towards to the Divine, will again be impossible to realize completely, but the striving after this recreation and direction is in itself right. However imperfect the result of necessity should remain, yet this task has to be entered upon wholeheartedly by those who are called unto it (whereas the Teacher himself seems to prefer keeping aloof): that result will no doubt be something better than the order now prevailing. Therefore we take the view that as the impulse imparted by the Teacher sinks in, a period of reawakening will also begin for the forms and that then all that has been proclaimed formerly as to the importance (although secondary) of ceremonies, the preponderance of the seventh ray and a period of the Holy Ghost[8] will come true completely. Then it will be the mission of the Theosophical Society, the Theosophical World-University, Co-Freemasonry, the Liberal Catholic Church, among other movements to influence and reform the world in the sense of the impulse imparted by Krishnaji.

Thus a fundamental contradiction becomes apparent by the problems we are discussing, Krishnaji choosing without hesitation the deepest of the two viewpoints (both of which are nevertheless partially true), while for obvious reasons neglecting the other. But other more concrete contradictions have been pointed out that seem to have to do with Plurality and about which it must be possible there fore to agree. Take *e.g.* the question of the apostles. It may be that we shall have to look upon the World-Teacher as being in other respects, *viz.* as a certain Adept, entrusted with a definite task relative to our world and its religions, as a somewhat more comprehensive being—a being comprehending especially more forms—than in his manifestation as Krishnamurti. This is a supposition explicitly suggested by Dr. Besant: "So far as we know, the consciousness of the World-Teacher enables Him to manifest through a material body of our own kind . . . only a very small part of that consciousness. . . .His material body does not share in the omniscience of the Lord Maitreya".[9] To this Krishnaji seems to have answered directly at Ojai saying: "Many of my friends are beginning to say: "We know him better elsewhere. It is only a part of his consciousness that is functioning".—How very childish these things are. . . Now I say I am whole—entirely unconditioned".[10]—This again seems hard to rhyme. But, when Krishnaji continually points to the formless, he represents, in sharp contrast to the world in which he fulfills his mission, the *highest aspect* of the Adept who ministers to the religious consciousness of mankind: that is where it is at one with the Father. But the Father is the totality of All, as against which all forms, including concrete knowledge, sink into nothingness. In so far as Krishnaji has realized in himself the Father—or the One Life, or the Beloved—, he is indeed everything, the Whole. This is again . . . a fundamental paradox. In consequence of that he is then at the same time, although sent out into this world of *coarse* matter, the *highest* aspect of the said Adept, with whom he has an intimate connection. This, however, need not prevent that same Adept comprehending more than Krishnaji in other, not higher, but lower, that is more formal aspects, and being not only the propagandist of the highest, godlike-onesided attitude towards life, but also insisting on other, more relative viewpoints. And in this other more formal respect, he has then already early laid the foundations on which the new impulse can operate in the midst of forms to direct them towards the divine. In so far certain persons and certain movements have been given by the World-Teacher a mission and indications all the same, though Krishnaji may never confirm this.

To take a general survey of all that is actually happening, we shall in this case have to consider not only Krishnaji, but also persons and movements about him. This whole group only constitutes as it were a microcosm inside which the insoluble and eternal antithesis of Life and Form, prevailing in the world, repeats itself. In 1928 it was still possible to suppose: at present Krishnaji speaks like this; later on he will speak differently to do justice to another aspect, that of form. The extreme individualism he is now preaching, will be later on compensated for by his pointing to the permanent value of the right form, as expressed for instance by the cooperation of the harmonious group or by a philosophic system that takes account of the formless. He may still do something of the kind. Then he will have to recall what he has said now. In that case the eternal fundamental paradox, the antithesis between Life and Form, which he is also powerless to eliminate, will be expressed *within* his doctrines. In the other alternative, which seems now more probable, he will continue to propagate only that highest aspect "to the end of my days". Then the eternal antithesis will work itself out within the *group* round about him, between himself and certain persons and movements *and* other persons and movements, that also profess allegiance to him; between his highest viewpoint and other principles that are also necessary and eternal.

Within the polarity of this antithesis each of us will finally have to find his or her place to the best of his or her ability, with the purest feelings and firmest resolution.[11]

November 1929

NOTES

[1] *Loc. cit.*, p. 296.

[2] *The Theosophist*, September 1928, p. 664.

[3] Whenever in this paper we mention the L.C.C., it is not because we consider it to be closely or necessarily connected with the Theosophical Society. But the form-aspect, which is not lacking in the latter either, is typically expressed in the L.C.C. and in so far it may be quoted as a speaking example.

[4] Unless what Dr. Besant writes in *The Watchtower* of October 1929, p. 4, is referred to: "...any apparent obscurity arises from the depth of the thought expressed...; great spiritual truths, rays of the One Truth, cannot be fully expressed in human language, developed on the lower planes of Being."

[5] *Tweeërlei Subjectiviteit*, p. 146; 392-393.

[6] Note in this connection the repetition of "According to my point of view".

[7] The antinomy of Life and Form is parallel to that of the Father and the Holy Ghost or of the transcendental (outside the world existing) and the immanent (inside the world working) Deity. An antinomy that can no more be solved in favour of one of the two terms than could the former: while the transcendent God is always the deepest, God works also for ever *within* the world. This is another eternal paradox. (Cp. *Tweeërlei Subjectiviteit*, p. 513-514).

[8] See J. J. van der Leeuw, *The Fire of Creation.*

[9] *The Theosophist*, February 1929, p. 463-464.

[10] *The International Star Bulletin*, July 1929, p. 7.

[11] The problems of the "coming" of the Teacher or not and contradictions involved have again become actual in the discussion round the pamphlet of E. L. Gardner: *There is no Religion higher than Truth*, 1963. Mr. N. Sri Ram, the present President of the Theosophical Society, wrote in *The Theosophist* of February 1964: "I would add to this sentence (obviously there has been no Coming, Gardner, p. 1) the words: 'as expected'" ... "May it not be that he (Krishnamurti) is fulfilling the mission to which the prophecy" (of A. Besant and C. W. Leadbeater) "really referred?". We quite agree with this suggestion of Sri Ram; and, as to the contradictions, they may be of an essential nature, as set forth above. One may add: the opposition of parāvidyā and aparāvidyā of the Vedānta shows likewise an essential and unavoidable contradiction. (Cp. also "Een felle bliksem?" *Theosofia*, June 1964, p. 189.)

IX

PSYCHOPHYSICAL PARALLELISM OR INTERACTIONISM?[1]

Which Provides the More Satisfactory Philosophical Background for Psychical Research?

Philosophy and the respective branches of science mutually influence each other. On the one hand, it is the duty of philosophy—besides its other tasks—to summarize the results of scientific research, forming a complete worldpicture. Thus philosophy accepts material from the other departments of knowledge. On the other hand, however, philosophy affects them: it considers the methods of science, and is able thereby to verify its results, and to discover fallacies in them. But there exists in a somewhat broader sense another dependence of the sciences upon philosophy: if philosophy has already arrived at distinct results, not only at such general and formal results as the laws of logic and methodology, but also at more material doctrines such as certain ideas on the essence of things and of reality, then philosophy will apply these ideas as a standard in judging new achievements of science. Since the results gained in a particular field should ultimately be in harmony with the conclusions of any other field, philosophy will entertain certain expectations concerning scientific developments; *a priori* it will consider one result to be more likely than another.

In this way, the philosophy of the nineteenth century, at the time when the views of natural science, tinged by materialism and positivism, had invaded its province to a great extent, showed little inclination to attach credit to the science of psychical research, which came into being at that very period. Since then, however, some changes have taken place: it is no longer possible to say that natural science, especially natural science of the nineteenth century, dominates philosophy. This fact has proved advantageous for psychical research (which is now called parapsychology more and more). But this does not mean that the influence of philosophy on psychical research has ceased altogether. The philosophical theories which prevail today have likewise taken a definite stand with regard to psychical research: certain results of psychical research are welcomed, and certain others rejected from the outset. All of this was to have been expected. Certain results, however, have already established themselves as facts so surely that any philosophy which takes account of experience will have to take them into consideration.

In this paper, I am going to pay special attention to a particular case where philosophy and a branch of science influence each other mutually: namely, the metaphysical theories concerning the relation of consciousness and body, spirit and matter on the one hand, and certain results of psychical research on the other. Among the phenomena of psychical research, some, like telepathy, have been proved real; some others, like clairvoyance or cryptaesthesia, can be placed almost in the same class; still others, including the survival after bodily death, are the subject of constant investigation. Now, which of the metaphysical theories concerning the relation of body and consciousness provides the best refuge for such doctrines of psychical research, partly proved today, partly to be proved tomorrow? In other words, to mention the two main rival theories by name: does a *Parallelism* with regard to psycho-physical relations, or does *Interactionism* provide the most useful background for psychical research?

Opinions are divided on this point. The philosopher W. McDougall gives as his opinion in his *Body and Mind* that psychical research may at any moment furnish the final verification of interactionism, or animism, as he calls it, and that already there has been established the occurrence of phenomena incompatible with parallelism or mechanism.[2] Other thinkers who have occupied themselves with the relation of philosophy and psychical research, like the well-known philosophers William James[3] and Henri Bergson[4]—each, like McDougall, was in his time President of the English S.P.R.—also adhere to the interactionistic view. The late Professor Gerardus Heymans, however, the founder and the first President of the Netherlands S.P.R., was of a wholly different opinion. He writes in an article *Psychischer Monismus und "Psychical Research"*[5] that precisely because of his "psychic monism" (which involves parallelism) he has been prejudiced in favor of psychical research; that there is in his metaphysical standpoint room for these phenomena from the outset; and even that by it he is able to predict the conditions under which they will appear.

Let us for a moment examine more closely this agreement between the theories and expectations of psychic monism and the results of psychical research. In what does this agreement consist? Psychic monism draws the analogy between our individual consciousness with its ideas on the one hand, and, on the other, a larger consciousness, perhaps a world-consciousness, within which the individual consciousnesses fulfill the function of ideas. Now, just as ideas may momentarily disappear from our consciousness, becoming memories which do not perish but can be recalled, so too, we as individual consciousnesses may disappear for the moment from a certain part of the world-consciousness, while surviving nevertheless in another part of it. From this analogy the likelihood of individual immortality follows, and also that of the possibility that the dead make themselves at some times and under special conditions known to us. Those special conditions have to be of such a kind that these impressions, whether they come from the deceased, or, as is the case with telepathy, from still living persons, can easily reach our consciousness. Therefor it is required that the consciousness of the recipient be not too much occupied by sense-impressions. One finds, as a matter of fact, that the trance of the medium and a certain passive state of the telepathist at least further the result, or may perhaps even be necessary.[6]

These considerations, which Heymans voices, referring explicitly to Fechner, seem to us to be very felicitous. Here a theory has been found into which a certain number of psychical phenomena fit from the beginning, and by which they therefore can so far be explained. Such a theory is not to be neglected. What strikes us, however, is that as a matter of fact nowhere in this analogy between the individual and a world-consciousness is there mentioned a parallelism between mind and body. Heymans uses the inferences following on this analogy as if they were the inferences "of psychic monism". Now, a very important part of psychic monism is the thought that the real is merely psychical, that therefore all the physical is essentially psychical, and merely physically *appears*. Nothing, or almost nothing,[7] however, of this part of the doctrine of psychic monism enters into the above-mentioned analogy, which enables us to explain certain psychic phenomena.

Much more, however, is said about that other part of psychic monism in the reflections on the relation of philosophy to psychical research of Professor Leo Polak, the successor of Professor Heymans at Groningen University, and, until some years ago, also as President of the Netherlands S.P.R. In his address *Feit en Hypothese* (Fact and Hypothesis) delivered at the Annual Meeting of the Netherlands S.P.R. in 1926, Professor Polak draws some concrete conclusions with regard to psychical research from the epistemological assumptions of psychic monism. He says among other things: "A spirit, who could move in space, be present in a body (either brain, or heart, or elsewhere), or step out of the body; thoughts, which could float in the air (in the literal sense!) and cover distances (with the swiftness of thought, too!) all this is equally absurd and contradictory as thought-reading or spirit-photos. . . Thoughts, as it is, can essentially never be read, that is, be perceived, but only be thought. And photos of spirit as such can never be taken".[8] Other utterances of Professor Polak, in his book *Kennisleer contra Materie-realisme*, can be compared with these: "If, for instance, Mr. F. van Eeden says in accordance with spiritualism . . . that in this room there may be no one knows how many spirits,—then we are able to reply with the apodictical apriorical certainty of epistemology: none whatsoever! *Ex hypothesi* in this room there can only be . . . matter!"[9] And further on: "Every spiritualizing of matter, or materialization of spirit, is a dogmatical superstition that can be accurately refuted as conflicting with epistemology (the immateriality of the spiritual, the ideality of space, the immanence of objects) and with the inviolability, based on epistemology, of the principles of natural science (the closed causality of nature, the conservation of energy)."[10]

So, as for the significance of psychic monism as regards the current results of psychical research, a considerable difference between the utterances of Heymans and of Polak, of master and of pupil, can be observed. A favorable reception, a seemingly *a priori* fitting of certain results of psychical research into the philosophical doctrine, on the one hand, is opposed to a strong distrust towards a number of psychical investigations that nevertheless deserve attention, and to a rejection on epistemological grounds of certain conceptions commonly used by psychical research, on the other.

We are inclined to acknowledge that Polak is right. We agree with him that there exists an unbridgeable gulf between certain provisional results of psychical research and the epistemological assumptions which cannot be separated from psychic monism. If some members of the Netherlands S.P.R. have had the impression that Professor Polak has sometimes been inclined to be too cautious in accepting facts, one cannot blame him overmuch for that. He has only been consistent. This is a case of bringing philosophical opinions to bear on a department of science, by which certain results of that science are held *a priori* to be or not to be likely. It is true that there is the possibility—as one of the debaters, Mr. P. Goedhart, remarked after the address of Professor Polak—"that the occult facts will prove that the philosophy of Professor Polak is not right".[11] In that case one would have to look for a different epistemology, in which the apparent results of psychical research would more easily come into their own. In that other epistemology there ought also to be a place for that analogy which Heymans draws between the individual and the cosmic consciousness. But it may very well be that Polak is perfectly right as regards the incompatibility of psychic monism, as an epistemological standpoint, with the results of psychical research. Because of this incompatibility, then, Polak has not been, as was Heymans, "favorably prejudiced" with regard to psychical research, but rather unfavorably prejudiced.

We are so far convinced that Polak is right with regard to the incompatibility of psychic monism with psychical research that we should like to take a step further. It is possible in our opinion to indicate within psychic monism, as Heymans conceived it, several points which it is very difficult to bring into line with certain results of psychical research, equally accepted or considered likely by Heymans. Heymans, then, overlooked these incongruities. If Polak ponders them, he will have to deny the reality of telepathy. Let us go into these points at some length.

The phenomenon of *telepathy*—our first point—has been proved, according to Heymans. The report of the investigation by Heymans, Brugmans and Weinberg states "that concerning the existence of thought-transference under conditions wholly excluding the ordinary intercourse through the medium of the senses all reasonable doubt has been set at rest".[12] Moreover, just as impossible as the intervention of the senses is the notion that there may be question only of an idea spontaneously arising in the mind of the percipient: that this is not so is demonstrated by the very fact of the agreement of the thought of the percipient with that of the experimenter. For the percipient the thought transferred undoubtedly comes from without. It comes as much from without as do the ordinary sensations. Now psychic monism assumes that the common sensations do not actually reflect the reality that is causing them. The human brain, *e.g.*, does not exist in itself; the contents of our consciousness, however, do exist in themselves, which thereupon appear as our brain to the eventual observer. A similar state of affairs is assumed by psychic monism for the whole of nature. *Can this be true?* one is inclined to ask. Reality in all ordinary cases is *not* adequately perceived, so that, for instance, if we avert our eyes from this desk, no brown wooden object remains, but only something psychical that *appears* to be of wood and brown, if one looks towards it—in all ordinary cases conditions are thus complicated; while in that rare and remarkable case, telepathy, then, the simplest possibility—that of appearing adequately—is real, for the thought of the experimenter agrees with the thought of the perceiver. It would be much more natural if there were in *both* cases either such a transmutation of the reality of qualities into appearance, or in *both* cases an adequate perception. Does not the intuitive conviction of our natural consciousness plead for the latter theory, according to which the qualities which we think we perceive really belong to the objects, such as this desk?

There are, accordingly, quite a few epistemologists who defend this adequacy of sense-perception, otherwise called Neo-realism. Now, conversely, Polak seems to agree with the requirement that, if psychic monism is true, there must be the same transmutation of qualities in the case of telepathy. He says in the above-mentioned address: "Thoughts, as it is, can essentially never be read, that is, be perceived, they can only be thought . . . and that only by their own subject; the thinking, therefore, of the thoughts of another person is, moreover, a contradiction".[13] Reading of the thoughts of another person, however, is nothing else than telepathy. So we agree with Polak, that, *according to psychic monism*, it is to be expected that thoughts, if they make themselves known to another consciousness, do not do so as thoughts, so that their own content is immediately caught, but in the form of appearances, which cannot be recognized without something further. According to Heymans, however, the reality of thought-transference has been proved. Consequently Polak, the consistent psychic monist, has either to deny the phenomenon of telepathy, or he has to alter his entire epistemology.

One might still suggest that in the case of telepathy the very factor which psychic monism holds responsible for the transmutation of the qualities, namely the distorting influence of our ordinary senses, has been ruled out. Telepathy may be said to be a transference of thought, not a different kind of perception. But, in the first place, Polak expresses himself strongly: "We are all, as a subject, monads without a window".[14] In other words: nothing that is content can penetrate into us from the outside: no more can thoughts. Secondly, one can point to other phenomena than telepathy. Little by little a sufficient number of cases of clairvoyance or cryptaesthesia have been proved real. Here also the very co-operation of the ordinary senses is excluded, but the content of which one becomes aware does not concern the thoughts of another person, but various objective events, which might, in principle, also be perceived by the ordinary senses. A perception which, as far as the content goes, is identical with sensory perception has, then, on the one hand been proved real in certain cases, and on the other been effected *without* the co-operation of the ordinary senses, which alone, according to psychic monism, can bring about the content of perception! Thus our conclusion upon reflection must be that facts like telepathy and clairvoyance cannot be reconciled with psychic monism. They form a direct contrary-instance against it.

Let us now pass on to a second point, with which both psychical research and psychic monism deal, and which likewise in our opinion involves a difficulty as regards the latter. It concerns a question which is important in psychical research: *the survival beyond bodily death.* Heymans, as we saw, considers this fairly probable because of reflections which he borrowed from Fechner. These reflections, however, had practically nothing to do, as we remarked, with the question of the parallelism between consciousness and brain. But if, on the other hand, one does connect this question of parallelism with that of death and eventual survival, then again, it seems to us, there are consequences which threaten psychic monism. One should bear in mind what, according to Heymans, is the point of departure of psychic monism. It is an empirical fact that there exists a certain parallelism between the processes of my consciousness and what is perceived (by another person) of my brain. In order to learn something about the unknown reality of things, one has, according to Heymans, to seize upon that very parallelism between the processes of my consciousness and the perceptions of my brain, for these processes of consciousness are immediately and certainly given to me, and the brain, too, is known only as a perception, that is, again, as a process of consciousness—of another, perceiving person. Therefore it is simplest to assume that the processes of consciousness themselves are the unknown reality manifesting itself in what is perceived of my brain. "Wenn aber irgendwo, dann (musz) jedenfalls hier das pou stô zu finden sein . . ., welches mir den Aufschwung in die unbekannte, in meinen Wahrnehmungen sich mir offenbarende Wirklichkeit gestattet".[15] From here the metaphysical theory of psychic monism with its epistemological presuppositions is built up. Apart from the circumstance that from the outset this wording, in our opinion, too readily assumes that it is an *unknown* reality that manifests itself in our perceptions—for the reality of things may as well lie in the qualities known to us—the relation between brain-phenomena and the processes of consciousness is in any case very important and essential. One wonders all the more that it seems possible to raise certain objections against psychic monism with regard to this very point of the narrow relationship between brain and consciousness. In the first place there is the case of fainting. Here the ordinary processes of consciousness cease. It is, however, likely that during this state the ordinary perceptions of the brain by another person should in principle still be possible. Consequently the direct relation, from which psychic monism started, has been disrupted in one instance at least.[16] The same applies still more plainly to that other phenomenon, death. In connection herewith L. Busse raises in his *Geist und Körper, Seele und Leib* the following objection against psychic monism: If our brain were, indeed, the appearance of our consciousness and nothing else, then, too, the decomposition of the body and of the brain after death would, at least to a certain extent, be an indication of what happens to our consciousness, and a slow, corresponding disintegration should occur there too.[17] One might add: Here is a new point of view as regards the choice between burial and cremation! Heymans, however, did assume, in contrast with these reflections, a certain personal survival, as we have seen. What, then, is his reply to this argument that there must needs be a parallel decomposition of body and of mind? "Dasz auch nach dem Tode das Gehirn nicht für die Wahrnehmung verschwindet, muss als ein Zeichen dafür angesehen werden, das im zugrunde liegenden Psychischen zwar die spezifisch-menschliche Gesetzlichkeit zurückgetreten ist, dafür aber eine allgemeinere und mehr primitive wieder die Oberhand gewonnen hat".[18] In other words, there is a parting of the ways between brain and consciousness at death. In that case one is, however, inclined to ask: what is left of the point of departure of psychic monism? Heymans started from the empirical parallelism between processes of consciousness and perceptions of the brain (by another person). The simplest theory, according to him, with regard to the relation of consciousness and body is, in connection with that empirical parallelism, that only the processes of consciousness are real, while the brain is merely an appearance in human perceptions thereof. The inference that the decay of the brain is an indication, at least to a considerable extent, of the fate of consciousness after death seems unavoidable. But now it suddenly appears that the brain is something else than merely an appearance of the processes of consciousness: a law, more primitive than that of man, again holds sway! It is true that one may construe these arguments in such a way that the primitive law, which got the upper hand, is also essentially psychical; and, conversely, Heymans expects that *physische Parallelerscheinungen*[19]—that corresponding physical phenomena might also eventually be demonstrated for the deceased, who are by that time independent of their brains.

But all becomes very complicated in this way. One thing is sure, anyway: Heymans has abandoned his point of departure, according to which my consciousness is simply mirrored in my brain. Meanwhile attention should be drawn to one point: if, as it appears from the parting of a specifically human and a more primitive law at death, the brain is *not* the *direct* appearance of the consciousness of man, but of something that is *connected* with his consciousness, then the whole conception becomes strikingly like the theory competing with parallelism: psycho-physical interactionism, assuming an action of consciousness on the brain—or on its substrate—and of the brain on consciousness. If one, then, considers that this transmutation of the qualities of things in perception (which is so awkward) is inseparably linked with psychic monism, then one begins to wonder whether an interactionism—without that transmutation—should not be preferred altogether.[20]

Our conclusion is, accordingly, that parellelism as the solution of the psycho-physical problem is hardly useful at all for psychical research. It is true that types of parallelism exist besides psychic monism, such as, *e.g.*, the "Theory of the Unknown Third" or Neo-Spinozism, and the "Theory of the Unknown Other"; but the general objections which Heymans raises against these standpoints as metaphysical doctrines seem to us insuperable.[21] Compared with them, psychic monism is much more flexible. But psychic monism appears to be irreconcilable with the results of psychical research. The transmutation of the qualities of things in perception is a lasting handicap to psychical research. If the results of this new science point in any direction, it is towards the existence of nothing else than a ready contact between the psychical and the physical, towards an influence of the psychical on the physical, much greater,[22] and much less dependent upon the ordinary senses, than used to be assumed. The theory of the inadequate appearance of things in perception hinders the establishing of these phenomena. In accordance with this Polak has drawn several conclusions from his epistemological point of view: thought-reading, spirit-photos, ghosts in this room are contradictory, essentially impossible. He ought to go on to say: the investigations of Heymans, Brugmans and Weinberg on telepathy are necessarily fallacious. As to the analogy, borrowed from Fechner, between the individual and world-consciousness, on account of which Heymans welcomes the results of psychical research, and is even able to predict the special conditions under which they will occur, this theory has practically nothing to do with psychic monism as a psychophysical parallelism and a doctrine of perception. One may as well include it in a different theory concerning the relation of consciousness and matter, *e.g.*, in an interactionism acknowledging the adequacy of perception. The fact that Polak is far less pleased with Fechner than Heymans is, tallies with all this. Polak reproaches Fechner expressly for not arriving at a correct theory of perception.[23] Polak has here been perfectly consistent; but it appears, on the other hand, that Fechner's analogy, on acccount of which Heymans welcomed psychical research, does not necessarily involve a rigorous doctrine of perception according to the recipe of psychic monism.

Now we might pass on to the inquiry as to whether an interactionism may perhaps be conceived, which is both satisfactory as a general metaphysical theory and yet meets the various objections raised by parallelism to the results of psychical reseacch. By way of introduction, we propose, however, first to examine the reasons why Polak adheres so strongly to his epistemological doctrine of perception—so strongly, in fact, that he is therefore even inclined *a priori* to deny the reality of a number of truly established facts of psychical research.

All sense-qualities are, says Polak, necessarily secondary: it is impossible for them to belong to things.[24] They cannot do so because, even if the content of sensation were a reproduction of the real qualities of the thing, we should never be able to know anything about any agreement between the two, since things themselves are never given to us, but only ideas, contents of consciousness indirectly caused by things. What is sometimes called "the third possibility of Trendelenburg" is out of the question. What are the three possibilities referred to? First, that we become directly aware of things, and therefore the qualities perceived belong to them. This first possibility, in our opinion as well, is out of the question; Polak rightly contends against Külpe and others that we never experience things themselves, but only ideas in connection with them. Consequently, says Polak, the second possibility is right, namely that we know merely the contents of our sensations, which are only the indirect effects of things possessing entirely different qualities in themselves. According to this theory the third possibility is impossible: that we only know, indeed, with regard to things the contents of our sensations, but that those sensations, nevertheless, contain the very qualities which belong to the things in themselves. We could never, he says, be aware of this agreement between the two; we are and we remain "monads without a window".

It seems to me that a way may yet be indicated whereby this difficulty could be removed and by which "Trendelenburg's third possibility", nevertheless, becomes possible and even likely. Allow me, therefore, briefly to repeat an argument which I worked out more elaborately in my book *Tweeërlei Subjectiviteit.* In epistemology one is accustomed to correlate the general judgments, going beyond the arbitrariness of the individual, empirical subject (such as the apriorical judgments with regard to space) with a supposed epistemological subject. This epistemological subject, however, is merely a supposition, hypothetical, an abstraction of the judgments of the empirical subjects. Now what about assuming that this general epistemological subject is *real?* By referring to self-consciousness I have tried to make it acceptable that such a general subject, which I have called the *suprasubject*—to be distinguished from the empirical subjects or *infrasubjects*—is actually real, of a profounder reality than common reality. In self-consciousness one may distinguish between a *differential I*, that is you and me, man or woman, having certain definite qualities and a distinct character, and a *pure I*. This "pure I" can never be completely objectified: if one tries to objectify it by the thought-experiment: "I think, that I think, that I think," *et cetera*, then this I, on the contrary, continually escapes the endeavor of objectification. One is never able to contemplate it *in front of* one, since it is present again and again as the subject in every new effort to know it. It is, therefore, according to experience that which escapes in principle, in other words the absolute; which means, does it not, that which is freed (absolvo). And this "pure I" is, notwithstanding these peculiar qualities, real; it is taken, as appears from the Cartesian *Cogito ergo sum*, as a very example of reality; also remember the saying: "As true as I live!" This "pure I", however, is to such an extent devoid of all concrete qualities that it is impossible to distinguish *many* pure I's; in other words there is only one pure I that thinks all thoughts in every one of us, being present at all ideas or contents of consciousness. In pure self-consciousness everyone encounters a reality profounder than that of the entire universe known to us, whether psychic or physical; it is the Absolute itself. If it should be so that all of us, in ourselves, may experience the One Pure I which is of a profounder than common reality, then by far the simplest way is to have it *coincide* with that one, general, epistemological subject which is needed in epistemology in view of the *a priori*. Consequently, however, the epistemological subject is also real, of a profounder reality than common reality.

The third possibility of Trendelenburg can be made acceptable in connection with this. For, *if* that epistemological subject to which the apriorical judgments are related, is at the same time the "pure I", being of a profounder reality than the entire remaining psycho-physical reality, one has to imagine that, on the one hand, from this one real suprasubject spring in reality the foundations and the laws of this entire lower psycho-physical world; whereas on the other hand, the suprasubject has planted a certain apriorical knowledge with regard to those foundations, *e.g.*, space or the scheme of colours, in the infrasubjects. If this be so, the *a priori* knowledge of the infrasubject and the qualities belonging to things themselves ultimately spring from the same source. Then the gulf between things in themselves and ourselves as infrasubjects has been *bridged*, though we may not experience things directly, but only the ideas caused by them in us. *Via* the suprasubject, which all of us have in ourselves as the "pure I", the infrasubjects are able to know something *objective* concerning the qualities of things, as these qualities spring from the same source, namely the basis of the world consisting of the one, real suprasubject or the "pure I", which, conversely, has also planted the apriorical knowledge of space or of the scheme of colours in us. And nothing but such an objectivity, such a true belonging of the qualities to things, is implied, according to phenomenology, if we consider something to be true; only such a theory satisfies and adequately accounts for our natural consciousness of what truth is.

It is entirely out of the question, therefore, that, as Polak will have it, the third possibility should be altogether inadmissible; that a theory of perception holding that qualities belong to things should be impossible, and that their transmutation should be necessary. The main reason for Polak's standpoint is probably the Kantian idea that we assimilate the data of our experience while adding something to them: space is *our conception (Anschauungsform)*. However, we admit wholeheartedly the existence of this apriorical knowledge together with the necessity of attributing it to the influence of a subject, since only in this way can its general, necessary and accurate character be explained. *One should, however, relate the apriorical knowledge to the suprasubject, and not to the infrasubjects.* Psychic monism, which says that this desk is really not brown and does not occupy any space, regards the *infra*subject as the source of the *a priori:* [25] it is the infrasubject which in its sensations conceives things in a spatial way: they, on the other hand, in reality and apart from it, are of a different nature. Polak says, absolutely in accordance with this standpoint, that it is impossible for ghosts to be in this room, that is, in this room regarded as a space. According to him it is, namely, the spirit of the infrasubject which actually creates space. We ourselves, as spirits, therefore, are not in this room. Conversely, all impressions from without have to undergo that spatial conception and transmutation, according to Polak. That is why he also says that thought-reading is essentially impossible. According to us, he is also forced to the conclusion that Heymans was mistaken in his experiments on telepathy. Thoughts, transmitted by telepathy, would *also* be transmuted. It is the same argument when Heymans remarks that it should be possible to demonstrate *physische Parallelerscheinungen*, corresponding physical phenomena of surviving persons, independent of the corpse.[26] And when Mr. Lissauer asked Professor Polak, in the discussion following his address on *Feit en Hypothese*, whether it was not possible that only the physical *appearance* of the spirits be present in the room, Professor Polak answered that in that case his objection would be removed.[27] In this way the intentions of psychic monism become clear.

This entire theory of perception, however, which by that transmutation of qualities causes so many difficulties (so that even the phenomenon of telepathy would have to be denied) is far from compelling. If one only relates the *a priori* not to the infrasubject but to the suprasubject, as we propose to do, a wholly different conception results, a simpler one, one in harmony with our natural consciousness of truth, whereas the main thought of Kantianism is retained, and psychical research rids itself of that awkward transmutation of the qualities. If the real source of the *a priori* lies in the one real suprasubject, if it is the suprasubject, and not the infrasubject, which posits space, and if it be true that the infrasubject assimilates the data of sensation, but only because of its relation to the suprasubject, then it is possible that spatial and other sense-qualities belong to things-in-themselves. In that case, however, quite another possibility exists too, namely that spatial qualities belong to things in a still broader sense: beyond the things of physical nature. *In that case the soul may also be seen as spatial and material.* I know very well that this seems to be a bold contention. But the results of psychical research, as stated above, point in the very direction of a ready contact between the psychical and the physical, making their affinity likely. The materialization of spirit, spirit-photos, and thought-reading suddenly re-enter the realms of possibility. The idea that man possesses yet another body, of a finer substance, has a respectable tradition behind it.[28] Nevertheless one will be inclined to raise serious objections to this conception. Let us review them calmly.

People will say "That is a *materialistic* conception". Yes, it would be a—dualistic—materialism, were it not true that in our theory the suprasubject or "pure I" is the profoundest existing reality. Materialism is the doctrine that matter is the profoundest reality. Our standpoint of hylic pluralism is, on the contrary, the purest idealism: the entire psycho-physical or hylic reality exists only as a less profound reality, if compared with the suprasubject, which has the whole psycho-physical reality before it as the general content of its consciousness (Bewusstseinsinhalt überhaupt).[29] This idealism is not changed, if one attributes spatial and material qualities to the soul in the same way as to physical nature.

Secondly, the objection might be raised that the soul is actually *immaterial*. But we do not intend to question immateriality as such. It goes without saying that there exists, *e.g.*, a certain immaterial relationship between a triangle and a square, or, more generally, that there exists something like one big immaterial coherence with regard to contents, independent of eventual material realization. This is true of the signification of physical nature, of the difference, for example, between ideal and real triangles. Consequently, neither is the signification *(der Sinn)* of *physical* nature material. Now one has to make the same distinction as regards psychical nature. The abstract *contents* of thought have to be distinguished from the real idea existing in a man's mind. Materiality and spatiality are only attributes of *the latter*, of real ideas. That big immaterial coherence or inner relationship between things *(the Eidetic)* is connected, in a way I cannot enlarge upon here, with the one suprasubject, which is real, but not material. So a distinction has to be made between the suprasubject or the immaterial spirit, and the psyche or the spatial and material soul.

Neither is it our intention to assign *only* material and spatial qualities to the soul, as, for a period, natural science used to attribute only form and matter, only geometrico-mechanical qualities to physical nature. No, in the same way as *all* our sense-qualities, colours and sounds included, can be attributed to physical nature, so, after one has laid the origin of the a *priori* in the suprasubject, can many more qualities in addition to the material ones belong to the soul.

If the reader persists in finding this conception of the soul a bit queer,[30] since one does not, as a rule, experience the contents of one's consciousness as something that fills space and is material, I may remind him of the following. Particularly in connection with psychical research this conception does not sound so uncommon, as, with regard to the phenomena of this science, there is question time and again, on the one hand, of material effects of thoughts or of "ideoplastics", on the other hand of a sort of clairvoyance, wherein that which as a rule remains subjective and closed is undoubtedly perceived as something objective and more or less spatial. Apart from that, one can point out that in ordinary cases as well the objectification—the simultaneously spatial perception—of *physical* objects has to be learned somewhere or other. Every baby acquires this faculty somewhere; it quite probably does not possess this faculty from the outset. People born blind never acquire it, any more, probably, than do a group of lower animals. Conversely, all of us already possess with regard to the *psychical* a certain sense of touch: we handle our ideas and feelings. There is, then, nothing absurd in the suggestion of an extension of this handling into their spatial perception.

Curiously enough, it can be pointed out that Heymans also has taken a view which seems to support these conceptions. In his paper *Über die Anwendbarkeit des Energiebegriffes in der Psychologie,*[31] Heymans answers the question whether energy can be attributed to the soul in the affirmative. As regards this psychical energy he elaborates from the data a set of notions, such as "potential energy", "energy of level", *et cetera*, of the contents of consciousness, and, in general, conservation of energy in this field as well. The resemblance to the potential energy of a physical body is obvious. Now Heymans, who is a psychic monist, means, of course, that only this psychical energy is real, while all physical energy is nothing but a reflection of psychical energy. He himself, however, points out the resemblance these results have to the physical law of gravitation, saying that "die Analogie mit räumlichen Bewegungsverhältnissen sich stets wieder aufdrängt" (the analogy with spatial conditions of motion repeatedly forces itself upon the mind).[32] Now one should consider that this investigation of his into psychical energy is, in itself, just as independent of psychic monism as a theory of the relation of body and mind, as is the above-mentioned analogy (borrowed from Fechner) between the individual and the world-consciousness. Obviously, then, one can say that Heymans has elaborated here, quite apart from psychic monism as a psycho-physical parallelism, which involves many difficulties, a theory about the soul which fits beautifully into a conception simply attributing not only its own, but also spatial and material qualities to the soul.

At this juncture, however, we must return to our point of departure: does parallelism or interactionism provide the more satisfactory philosophical background for psychical research? We have seen that parallelism certainly does not fulfill this requirement, as the most felicitous parallelistic theory, psychic monism, involves a great number of difficulties as regards psychical research. As far as psychophysical interactionism is concerned, we may now fairly quickly arrive at a conclusion. As said in the beginning, James, Bergson and McDougall believed in a relation between psychical research and interactionism. This is only to be expected, as psychical research deals constantly with independent workings of the soul, either during man's life or during his eventual survival after death. Body and soul cannot, then, be as closely related as parallelism contends they are. But all interactionistic theories so far possess one great shortcoming: they are not in a position to explain the *influxus:* the actual interaction between soul and body. The reason is that they still contain remnants of the old Cartesian dualism of soul and body: the soul is immaterial, the body is material; how can two such heterogeneous substances possibly act one on another? It is clear, however, that as soon as one draws the dividing line between the immaterial and the material in another way, namely not between the psychical and the physical, but between the psychical and the One spirit or the suprasubject, then the heterogeneity of the psychical and the physical at once disappears to make way for an all-round homogeneity, by which the influxus suddenly ceases to be inconceivable.

This is no place to enter into all the details of such an interactionism. Its probability has to be carefully compared with that of a theory of parallelism. It appears, then, that interactionism and not psychic monism supplies the simplest formula whereby the three laws in question can be explained: of psychical, of physical and of psycho-physical phenomena.[33] I may refer to my book for details on these matters. I would like to remark, however, that neither can the objections raised in connection with the closed causality of nature be raised against *this* interactionism: the soul also belongs to nature, and a transmission of energy can take place. For the rest I want to conclude my paper with the following: just as some rare phenomena like the attraction of rubbed amber and the convulsions of a dead frog's leg developed into the theory and practice of modern electricity, so the present investigation into psychic phenomena will, very likely, lead to big things. Psychical research has a brilliant future in store, but in view of that future development psychical research needs a fruitful philosophical background. In my opinion it wants, where the relation of soul and body is concerned, not a parallelistic but an interactionistic theory, emphasizing psycho-physical homogeneity.[34]

NOTES

[1] Address to the Annual Meeting of the Netherlands S.P.R. at Utrecht, May 8th, 1932. See *Journal of the American S.P.R.*, Febr. 1937; *Tijdschrift voor Parapsychologie*, IV, p. 214 *seq.*; *Variaties...*, p. 47 *seq.*; *Zeitschrift für Parapsychologie*, VIII (1933), p. 510 *seq.*

[2] P. 348-349.

[3] *Principles of Psychology*, Vol. I, p. 181.

[4] Cp. *Fantômes des Vivants* and *Recherche psychique* in *L'Energie spirituelle.*

[5] *Zeitschrift für Psychologie*, Vol. 64, 1-2, p. 1 *seq.*; *Gesammelte Kleinere Schriften*, Vol. I, p. 341. *seq.*

[6] Cp. Heymans, "Over de verklaring der telepatische verschijnselen", in *Mededeelingen der Nederlandsche S.P.R.*, Vol. 10, p. 1, *seq.*

[7] *Zeitschrift für Psychologie*, Vol. 64, p. 10.

[8] *Mededeelingen der Nederlandsche S.P.R.*, Vol. 12, p. 19.

[9] P. 79-80.

[10] P. 334.

[11] *Mededeelingen Nederlandsche S.P.R.*, Vol. 12, p. 27.

[12] *Mededeelingen Nederlandsche S.P.R.*, Vol. 1, p. 6.

[13] *Mededeelingen Nederlandsche S.P.R.*, Vol. 12, p. 19.

[14] *Ibidem*, p. 14.

[15] *Einführung in die Metaphysik auf Grundlage der Erfahrung*, § 31; *Der Grundgedanke des psychischen Monismus*, p. 226. If anywhere, then here at all events one should be able to find the startingpoint which affords the transition into the unknown reality behind my perceptions.

[16] Cp. *Tweeërlei Subjectiviteit*, p. 277-279, 281.

[17] P. 372-376.

[18] *In Sachen des psychischen Monismus*, Part V, p. 212: *Gesammelte Kleinere Schriften*, Vol. I, p. 355. That after death the brain does not vanish for perception, is an indication that in the underlying psychical the specifically human laws were withdrawn indeed, whilst more general and primitive laws again prevail.

[19] *Gesammelte Kleinere Schriften*, Vol. I, p. 355.

[20] After the writing of the above we came across the text of an address *Le sens de la mort*, delivered by Professor Polak on Feb. 23, 1928, at Paris (*Union pour la Vérité, Bulletin*, 39e année, 2-3, nov.-déc. 1931, p. 41). Dealing with *le monisme psychique* and its epistemology, based on Kant, Polak says here: "Pour cette théorie l'unité de l'organisme vivant est le phénomène, l'indice de l'unité du moi pensant, de l'individu psychique,—et la décomposition de cet organisme est à la fois l'effet et la preuve de la désintégration de ce moi particulier, subjectif, individuel, sa désindividualisation finale" (p. 50). And further on: "Ainsi la mort physiologique (en opposition à la mort pathologique, prématurée) c'est la fin normale et définitive de toute existence individuelle" (p. 51).

These utterances confirm in an unexpected way our arguments, namely, that a consistent psychic monist not only has to disavow the phenomenon of telepathy (which Polak already does with more or less clarity in his address *Feit en Hypothese*), but also, because of the decomposition of the organism after death, is obliged to deny every personal survival after death. It follows that the present professor of philosophy at Groningen University and his predecessor largely disagree with regard to these two points. Nevertheless in our opinion Polak is right in his inferences from psychic monism. But it seems very doubtful to us that these inferences, including the impossibility of personal immortality, should follow directly from Kantianism, and, indeed, this has only very rarely been maintained. Therefore a theory of knowledge, especially of perception, differing from the one on which psychic monism is based is necessary, and it is, we think, possible. In as much as the phenomena of psychical research become corroborated as the years go by, there will be a decision between these two epistemologies.

[21] Cp. Heymans, *Einführung in die Metaphysik*, § 22, § 27.

[22] Cp. W. H. C. Tenhaeff, "Ideoplastie" in *Tijdschrift voor Parapsychologie*, Vol. III, p. 216 *seq.*

[23] *Kennisleer contra Materie-realisme*, p. 178.

[24] Cp. *e.g.* "Feit en Hypothese", *Mededeelingen Ned. S.P.R.*, Vol. 12, p. 15.

[25] It may be pointed out, however, that Heymans does not seek the origin of the apriorical knowledge as regards time and causality in the infrasubject, but in the World-being, that is, in something like our suprasubject. We propose to extend this conception to *all* forms of the *a priori.*

[26] "Psychischer Monismus und 'Psychical Research'," *Ges. Kl. Schriften*, Vol. I, p. 355.

[27] *Mededeelingen Nederlandsche S.P.R.*, Vol. 12, p. 28.

[28] Cp. W. H. C. Tenhaeff, *Beknopte Handleiding der Psychical Research*, I: "Het Astraallichaam"; G. R. S. Mead, *The Doctrine of the Subtle Body in Western Tradition*; the author's *Ochêma.*

[29] Polak's requirement, the immanence of the object, remains satisfied in this way, no longer as regards the infrasubject, but, as a matter of fact, as regards the suprasubject.

[30] Wilhelm Haas expounds similar ideas in his *Die psychische Dingwelt* (1921).

[31] *Gesammelte Kleinere Schriften*, Vol. II, p. 319 *seq*.

[32] *Loc. cit.*, p. 340.

[33] Cp. *Tweeërlei Subjectiviteit*, § 49.

[34] The problems dealt with in this paper are now much less in the limelight than in the days of Heymans, McDougall and Bergson. The standpoint of existentialists and phaenomenologists is that consciousness and body, the psychical and the physical form a sort of natural unity. This is the general feeling in reaction to the dualistic standpoint of Descartes and his followers. But even if this be so (and we largely agree), the nature of the relation between the two should be clearly stated. If psychophysical parallelism has almost completely been abandoned, interactionism comes to the fore. What kind of interactionism? According to us, an exchange of energy between the psychical and the physical takes place; the nature of the psyche is (in opposition to the One Spirit or nous) of a subtle materiality as contended by "hylic pluralism".

X

"THE INDIVIDUAL PROBLEM IS THE WORLD-PROBLEM"[1]

It seems to me:

1. That the meaning of the phrase often used by Mr. Krishnamurti: *The Individual Problem is the World-Problem*, as commonly understood by Star-People and Theosophists, is the following: When one wishes to change conditions in the world, start with the alteration, improvement and liberation of the individual. Then the world will change accordingly.
2. That the natural way of expressing this opinion is: The World-Problem is the Individual Problem.
3. That therefore the way, in which Mr. Krishnamurti and others put it, is misleading. Nobody seems to have noticed this so far, because everyone concerned agrees as to the exact reverse of what is being said.

In some languages a sentence can be begun with the predicate, which in these cases is nevertheless clear, as either the case (*e.g.* of the article) indicates its position, or the verb precedes the subject, the two belonging apparently together, or by the way of stressing the first word, or in all these ways at the same time (*e.g.* in German: *Den Mann kennen wir schon lange)*. But neither of these possibilities exists or is correct in English. So in the phrase of Mr. Krishnamurti "The Individual Problem" must be the subject, "the World-Problem" the predicate.

In logic we learn that of the two terms of a judgment the term of the predicate is as a rule the larger one (*e.g.* "Socrates is a man"), though in some rare cases the extent of the terms may be the same, but the extent of the term of the subject is never larger than that of the term of the predicate. Now the meaning of the phrase, upon which all people agree, is exactly that the individual problem not only has its own value, but is also the key to the world-problem and not the reverse, that the individual problem can only be solved in and through the world-problem.

So the phrase cannot be correct, and it is good to draw attention to the fact to avoid misunderstanding in the future.

A question regarding this point was sent in at the Ommen-Congress of 1931, but was not answered.

[1] See *The Theosophist*, June 1932 (LIII, 2), p. 331.

XI

THE FEELING OF BEING STARED AT[1]

It is contended that a person can be compelled to look round merely by someone staring at him; conversely, that people sometimes get the impression that they have looked round only because they were being stared at from behind or from aside. As there seems to be no explanation of this supposed phenomenon along the lines of ordinary sense-experience, the matter should be studied by parapsychology. The writer has been interested in this matter for a long time. In the *Tijdschrift voor Parapsychologie* 1939, vol. 11, p. 97 *seq.* he published a lengthy paper on it.[2] He wishes to summarize the contents of that paper here while adding some new considerations.

First of all, some people were interviewed by him with regard to this contention. Quite a number of them declared that they had had such an experience themselves. Dr. (now Professor) E. R. told him, for instance, that one day he had been sitting in a concert hall. He had had no desire to look round. Suddenly he felt the urge to look round, and thereupon looked a Mr. X. whom he knew in the face. During the interval he went to Mr. X. and asked him about it. Mr. X. said that he had not looked at Dr. R. before that particular moment, and that he had not been surprised that Dr. R. actually looked round. Dr. R. concluded that what had happened was "absolutely convincing".

The writer himself has also experienced the phenomenon. For instance, it has so often happened to him that, when walking down a street, he suddenly felt the impulse to look at a certain window, and that it then appeared that there was a person looking at him from there, that he cannot reasonably doubt the genuineness of the phenomenon. It was especially the swiftness of his own reaction, the certainty of the direction in which he had to look up, and the attitude of the person looking (still staring, or drawing back, feigning not to have looked at all) that gave him food for thought. The facts that the two events, his looking up and the other person's looking down, repeatedly go together, while no other factor is repeated; and that in addition there was a strict contiguity both in time and space (direction!), give a strong impression of the existence of a causal connection between them. All this would fall under the "Joint Method of Agreement and Difference" of John Stuart Mill and G. Heymans. To be sure such an impression remains subjective and constitutes no objective proof. But introspection has a certain value, at least a heuristic value, and can provide a starting point.

With regard to his own experiences the writer has noticed some special features. He is predominantly passive and but rarely active in this connexion. When he is the agent, the phenomenon occurs more readily, when he is staring at a person, while he himself is at the same time deep in thought (for instance, while staring out of a window after he has read something interesting and exciting). Now all this is covered by the observation that "the more one tries, the less one succeeds". This rule does not apply to ordinary routine-matters, but especially to the finer achievements of life (such as writing poetry; inventing leading thoughts, and so on); they cannot be forced, they come of their own accord at unexpected moments, while the other half of the mind is busy with unimportant things. One might call this valuable concentration *second-degree attention*, while at the same time the rest of one's attention is focussed on common things.[3] Such situations are not altogether unknown in psychical research or parapsychology. In a paper: *La télépathie, ses rapports avec le subsconscient et l'inconscient*, Mr. Warcollier has pointed out that the role of *le mal perçu*, of that which is hardly perceived, is considerable in telepathy.[4] The late Whately Carington agreed with all this. In a letter of March 1940 he wrote to the author of this paper: "I suspect that the more one concentrates the less well one does! It seems to be those who take the job quite lightly (though not frivolously) who do best". Experiments of von Neureiter with Ilga K. seem to confirm the existence of the same tendency.[5]

So there is no reason to be surprised that the feeling of being stared at shows the same feature. Conversely, it makes the parapsychological nature of the phenomenon seem more likely. Meanwhile, it certainly does not facilitate experimenting with it. It may explain the negative result of a set of experiments John Edgar Coover of Leland Stanford Jr. University conducted on the phenomenon years ago.[6] Coover's negative outcome may have been the reason that parapsychologists did not see any problem in it after that. But the way Coover carried out the experiments is in the writer's opinion open to criticism. Though Coover selected among his students those who declared they had had experience of the phenomenon, his agent was not chosen carefully enough, and the staring-time was too short. For half of the experiments Coover himself functioned as the agent. Who can tell that he was the right person for that, in possession of the seemingly rare faculty of being able to cause another person to look round? It seems that the difficulty is to obtain a concentration deep enough to have an effect on the percipient, a concentration which may be achieved, when one stares while musing on absorbing and important matters. As a rule, the percipient's back is not the most interesting part of him. Anyhow, 15-20 seconds' staring strikes one as being very short.

Before reporting on the experiments—admittedly too few—that the writer conducted on the matter himself, he will go into some more considerations concerning the problem.

It may be of some significance from the heuristic point of view that the writer believes he has experienced the feeling of being stared at while the other, the active person, looked at him via a mirror. So, if any rays are involved, they behave to a certain extent in the same manner as light-rays. However, the writer thinks he has observed yet another phenomenon: when walking in a street or sitting in a tram it sometimes happens that one has the urge to look up at a person, of whose presence one is already aware without looking at him, and that the other person then also looks up suddenly. In such cases neither was looking at the other. Whether the urge originated in A or in B, one again gets the strong impression of a causal connection. But in such cases staring cannot have been the cause. If both kinds of looking up are facts and are kindred, they might both be of a purely telepathic nature.

The writer has written to several Institutes for the Blind, asking whether it had been noted there that blind people were susceptible to the gaze of others purposely looking at them. The answers were negative. But in the case of the blind sight is entirely eliminated, and so, it seems, also the influence of active staring. If they have, as has been contended, as sixth sense, then this does not seem to be connected with their eyes.

It is remarkable that in many novels the feeling of being stared at is described. The writer and some others who helped him noted no less than eighty-six passages in which this was done, and the authors concerned were very well-known ones such as: Tolstoy, Dostoievsky, Anatole France, Galsworthy, Victor Hugo, Aldous Huxley, D. H. Lawrence, F. Mauriac, M. Mitchell, Ch. Morgan, J. Cowper Powys, J. B. Priestley, R. Rolland, H. Walpole, F. Werfel, Th. Mann and many others. What can one make of this? The very character of fiction comes much to the fore, if the author is inclined to indulge in romantic or more or less occult descriptions, as was the case, for instance, with Victor Hugo and J. Cowper Powys. But if the phenomenon is mentioned in novels of a perfectly natural, realistic character, with no tendency to be mysterious or occult, one might say this: either the author assumes the phenomenon to be real and a matter of common knowledge to a keen observer, or he makes the mistake of inserting something that strikes a false note. Authors such as Galsworthy,[7] M. Mitchell,[8] H. Walpole[9] and many others would never have done such a thing. So the matter really rests with the author. The writer has corresponded with several of them, when they were still living. In their answers some were vague, others, however, were very positive. Aldous Huxley replied: "I have often had the sensation of being stared at and, looking up, found it to be a fact." One should also bear in mind that the phenomenon has been so little investigated or commented upon that it may hardly have become a "hobby" of all these novelists. They seem to have inserted it straight from practice.

One is also reminded of the superstition of *the evil eye* which attributes some power to the eyes of certain persons. The belief in it is incredibly widespread throughout the history of mankind. Dr. S. Seligmann of Hamburg went into this subject in a large work, in which he sums up the occurrence in many civilizations in diverse ages.[10] The belief is obviously of a strongly superstitious nature, but it is certainly deeply rooted. One wonders if the explanation of the evil eye might be that the phenomenon of looking up when being stared at is genuine and common enough, and so may have occasioned the superstition.

It is curious that already Democritus of Abdera tried to explain the working of the evil eye by a theory that something is emitted by the eye when a man looks: i.e. the *eidola*. According to him the eidola of the jealous reach the envied person, stay with him and vex him.[11] In antiquity yet other thinkers held that in the act of looking something goes forth from the eye. In Plato's opinion a current of fire leaves the eye and meets another current coming from the objects.[12]

Some modern occultists, such as Inayat Khan and Geoffrey Hodson,[13] also teach the exteriority of sight.

It should also be mentioned that some investigators have maintained that inanimate objects could be influenced by looking at them. Paul Joire[14] and Charles Russ[15] were active in this direction. The results of their experiments, however, do not seem to be convincing. But one should bear in mind that at least one effect of human eyes seems to have been proved: the mitogenetic rays, discovered by A. Gurwitsch, however weak they may be.[16]

We now come back to the experiments of the power of the eye in a stricter sense, i.e. to those concerning the feeling of being stared at. Dr. Seligmann tells us in the second edition of his book on the evil eye of some primitive experiments performed in Paris. An officer of the criminal police made five constables, who were said to possess a magnetic look, gaze at a row of ten soldiers through a small hole, with the result that some of the latter suddenly looked in the direction of the hole.[17] Among scientific researchers, apart from Coover, the American psychologist E. B. Titchener has occupied himself with the matter. The outcome of his experiments was negative.[18] Consequent upon his own introspective observations the present writer nevertheless believes that experiments are worth-while and promising.

The set-up of Coover's tests does not seem bad. Dice were thrown to decide whether the agent should look or not; every time the dice had come to rest the leader tapped the table with a pencil and the percipient had to say yes or no. The result of about 1000 experiments was very poor: 50.2% right answers which is about chance.

The writer tried a series of experiments with Mrs. W. A. L. R.—V. (member of the City Council of The Hague; who died in 1948). She had told him that she resorted to staring at a person whom she saw at a gathering and to whom she wished to speak.

The writer himself—being passively sensitive—acted as percipient. The result of 89 experiments was as follows:

TABLE

Date	*Right*			*Wrong*			*Total*
	yes/yes	*no/no*	*Total*	*yes/no*	*no/yes*	*Total*	
27-4-'38	3	—	3	—	—	—	3
19-5-'38	2	3	5	1	1	2	7
31-5-'38	4	1	5	2	1	3	8
14-6-'38	1	2	3	3	2	5	8
28-11-'38	3	2	5	1	1	2	7
1-12-'38	2	3	5	1	1	2	7
28-2-'39	1	5	6	2	3	5	11
6-3-'39	2	2	4	3	3	6	10
27-4-'39	3	5	8	4	3	7	15
10-5-'39	3	6	9	1	3	4	13
Total	24	29	53 = 59.55%	18	18	36 = 40.45%	89

Agent yes: 24+18=42
Agent no: 29+18=47

Total:

Percipient yes: 24+18=42
Percipient no: 29+18=47

This result of 59.55% right answers proved to be better than Coover's 50.2%, but was not yet satisfactory. In a letter of 21 May 1939 W. Whately Carington called the writer's figures "suggestive and highly promising, but they do not achieve significance". It is quite obvious that the number of experiments was far too low. But it was difficult to get hold of Mrs. R. and after a time the experiments had to be stopped altogether. It may be remarked that, if one takes the results of the three first sessions separately, the outcome is far better: 13 experiments right and 5 wrong, or 72.22% and 27.78%. A decline in the number of positive results after the start has also been observed elsewhere.

The writer wishes to make a strong appeal to parapsychologists who are specialists on experimental lines to make new attempts to establish whether any ESP can be proved with regard to the feeling of being stared at.

In conclusion a few remarks of a theoretical nature will be made. The phenomenon, if genuine, strikes one as forming a kind of *transition* between ordinary and extrasensory perception. One of the senses is involved: *sight;* there is a relation with *direction;* a mirror might be able to convey the influence. If the theory of rays of a subtle nature seems hardly sound elsewhere, here there is almost "phenomenological" evidence of them.

On the other hand, one has to remember Whately Carington's explanation of telepathy. According to him associations can work, when an idea A is in the mind of a person P and the other idea B is within the mind of a person Q, provided that the two minds have a K-idea in common.[19] Now staring certainly means that the idea of the body of the percipient is a lively image in the mind of the agent, and the percipient no doubt has at all times a lively and susceptible image or idea of his own body. So the phenomenon of looking up while being stared at may actually be telepathic. If the writer be correct in thinking that a second person can sometimes be made to look up without looking at him by the more or less, but rather less, conscious urge to have contact with him (see above page 110), then that seems also to indicate that the association theory is right, and not a theory involving rays. But might it not, in this case, be indicated to subsume even "ordinary perception" under the association theory?

Postscript

The Editor of the *Journal of the S.P.R.* has asked for more details concerning the experiment. The sessions took place at the house of the agent, Mrs R. There were no other people present besides the agent and the percipient. The percipient was seated with his back to the agent who sat in the second room of a suite. The percipient knocked in order to call attention to the fact that a particular trial was going to start. The agent knocked to signify that she also was beginning. She then took a card from an ordinary pack of playing cards which had been well shuffled. If a red card was turned, she began staring at the percipient; if the card was black, she avoided looking at him. The duration of her stare was first 3-5 minutes, at the later trials 2-3 minutes. There were no regular intervals kept between the trials. Both participants made notes; the agent whether she had stared or not; the percipient whether the agent, according to him, had stared or not. The trials were numbered. Both added remarks if they seemed necessary. Results were compared after the session; sometimes in the midst of a session. The percipient watched the time, and waved his hand, or said so, when it was time to break off, and he then wrote down his result. A final knock of his ended the particular trial.

Were there any signs of post- or precognitive effects? We figured that out on the basis of the results. As sometimes considerable time elapsed between successive sessions, we only investigated the respective sessions with a view to this, not the series of the trials as a whole. This gives 79 results to be taken into account, as either the first or the last trial drops out. Moreover, the whole session of 19 May 1938 was left out, as in the midst of it a trial had had to be cancelled. In this case, namely, the agent had noted "black", but "I looked nevertheless a fragment of a second at the start". The percipient had, curiously enough, noted in this case: "an impulse to look round, especially in the first minute", therefore: "yes". There remained 73 cases to be looked into with a view to post- or precognitive effects. The results are that 44 postcognitive relations were right (18 yes-yes, 26 no-no), 29 wrong. This gives 60.3% of right relations, which is almost the same percentage (59.55%) of the normal trials. Of possible precognitive relations 38 were right and 35 wrong, which is about in accordance with chance: 52% right answers. Of the 38 right answers 16 were here yes-yes, 22 no-no. So in general the right answers no-no were in the majority. In the case of possible postcognitive effects the answers no-no formed 59% of the right answers.

The writer wishes to stress that his trials have only the value of a preliminary attempt. Obviously the number of them was far too small, and more precautions, such as looking through glass-panes, ought to have been taken. Mrs. R., a very busy person, was no longer inclined to continue the trials in which she was not very interested.

NOTES

[1] See *Journal of the Society for Psychical Research* (London), Vol. 40, Part 699, March 1959, p. 4 *seq.*

[2] See also *Variaties...*, p. 129 *seq.*

[3] Cp. our *Het Hegemonikon en zijn Aandacht van den Tweeden Graad*, Assen 1939 and in *De Grondparadox*, p. 141 *seq.*

[4] *Revue Métapsychique*, Vol. 10, 1929, p. 277.

[5] F. von Neureiter, *Wissen um fremdes Wissen auf unbekanntem Wege erworben*, Gotha 1935.

[6] J. E. Coover, "The feeling of being stared at—experimental", *American Journal of Psychology*, Vol. 24, 1913, p. 570 *seq.*; idem, *Psychical Research Monograph*, Vol. I, 1917, p. 144-67.

[7] J. Galsworty, *The Man of Property*, p. 351.

[8] M. Mitchell, *Gone with the Wind*, p. 179.

[9] H. Walpole, *The Secret City*, p. 425.

[10] S. Seligmann, *Der böse Blick und Verwandtes*, Berlin 1910; idem, *Die Zauberkraft des Auges und das Berufen*, Hamburg 1922.

[11] E. Zeller, *Die Philosophie der Griechen* I, p. 839: in *Plutarch*, Symp. V, 7, 6 par. 682 F. (Cp. C. J. de Vogel, *Greek Philosophy* I, p. 74).

[12] Plato, *Timaeus*, XVI, 45 B-46.

[13] In *World-Theosophy*, I, 7, p. 513.

[14] P. Joire, "Etude de la force nerveuse extériorisée et enregistrée par le sténomètre", *Revue de l'hypnotisme*, February 1905.

[15] Ch. Russ, "An instrument that is set in motion by vision or the proximity of the human body", *The Lancet* 1921, p. 222 *seq.*, p. 308 *seq.*, p. 361 *seq.*

[16] A. G. Gurwitsch, *Mitogenetic analysis of the excitation of the nervous system*, Amsterdam 1937.

[17] See note 10: 1922 p. 323.

[18] E. B. Titchener, "The feeling of being stared at", *Science*, Vol. 8, 1898, p. 895 *seq.*

[19] W. Whately Carington, *Telepathy*, London 1945, Ch. VI.

XII

ARE A NEW PRESENTATION OF THEOSOPHY AND A NEW ATTITUDE NEEDED?[1]

In a couple of articles DR. A. G. VREEDE has given his opinion concerning several points which are of essential importance to the Theosophical movement. They are entitled: *We Need a New Presentation of Theosophy*[2] and *A New Attitude.*[3] The need exists, the writer says, as the work in many Lodges has dried up; Theosophy seems to have become a "closed system".[4] Now this is obviously a matter which concerns all Theosophists and which should be given careful consideration. Therefore, we should like to make a few remarks on the subject.

The Theosophical Society is not a spiritual trend possessing dogma's. If it has become a "closed system", that would be wrong. One should maintain an open mind. To the individual this is so far-reaching a demand that it is likely to cause him to abandon a movement which he feels he has outgrown.

To what extent can a movement change, yet remain the same? This will depend on the wording of its objects. If the latter are broad, considerable change and growth will be possible. The Theosophical Society would, however, no longer be itself, if a pronouncement concerning the superiority of a certain race were inserted in its First Object. Other trends and ideologies have far more rigid objects or tenets. If archaeological findings should prove that G.R.S. Mead was right in contending that Jesus lived about 100 B.C., the theological edifice of the R.C. Church might very well shake, though its adherents would not necessarily become atheists as a result. The point at issue, therefore, is to what extent a movement can transform itself and still remain the same and a unity.[5]

Within the Theosophical movement taken in a slightly broader sense something of the kind has already occurred. The Society under the leadership of Mrs. Tingley used to voice the opinion that it was more faithful to the teachings of Mme Blavatsky than the Society with Dr. Besant at its head. The first Society even called the Theosophy taught by Dr. Besant and Mr. Leadbeater "Neo-Theosophy". In this connection one need not even think of the so-called coordinated movements (The Order of the Star in the East; Co-Masonry; the Liberal Catholic Church and so on), but of the teachings from "The Secret Doctrine" elaborated in the well-known Manuals on the various planes and in other more lengthy publications. At the same time members of the Adyar-Society strongly felt that this elaboration was no deviation from the teachings of Mme Blavatsky, but rather an enrichment of them.

The assessment of such an elaboration depends on what is considered to be essential and of lasting value, and on the degree of insistence behind it. Are the new ideas justified, because they have hitherto been neglected, though they were implicitly present all the time, or did thought outside the movement develop along lines which cannot be ignored? [6]

Dr. Vreede has brought several points to the fore that are of some consequence. We enumerate the following four. 1) *The feminine side* of creation has been neglected.[7] Dr. Besant, too, gives a masculine description of the Deity; this amounts to a one-sided presentation, an inveterate masculine attitude.[8] 2) Theosophists have not kept pace with the development of science, which is now proclaiming among other things, that the *law of cause and effect* has a merely statistical character.[9] 3) *The "I"* has been too much concentrated upon; the subject-object method is wrong.[10] 4) A *functional* attitude should replace a static attitude.[11]

Let us consider *Point 2* first. It is correct that physicists have come to the conclusion that rigid causal laws cannot be applied to certain phenomena and that nothing but statistical law can be arrived at there. In principle one cannot tell how a particular particle, an electron for instance, will behave, whether it will disintegrate now or much later. Some physicists have drawn a conclusion which goes a great deal farther, a conclusion which, as a matter of fact, is of a philosophical nature, *viz.*, that the law of causality no longer holds good. There has been opposition to this conclusion. No less a person than Einstein has declared that he did not want to drop causality so quickly.[12] These problems are really too complicated to deal with exhaustively in this paper. We can refer the reader to another of our publications, where more is said about these problems. There we pointed out that one should certainly distinguish whether it is possible to predict certain phenomena precisely, or whether they are not determined *in themselves*.[13] In other words: there may be a difficulty with regard to their knowledgeability, but causality in itself in connection with them may very well exist all the time. Other writers, Professor A. G. M. van Melsen of Nijmegen University for instance, have come to similar conclusions.[14] Nowadays science, more particularly nuclear physics, shows a tendency in a certain direction. Its tendency may change some years hence. One should not meddle too lightly with such a deep and universal law as causality. A Theosophist should hesitate here for two reasons. As the law of Karma (often simply called the "Law of Cause and Effect") Theosophy teaches a far more extended validity of the causal law than the Occident as a rule does. If someone dies in an accident, then causal factors are not only the physical circumstances (speed; slipperiness of the road), but the further consequences to the life-work of the victim and to the economic position of his wife and children were also effects of preceding causes, though they may lie in the distant past. It will not be easy to know these exactly. Nevertheless Karma is considered by theosophists to be actual. If one agrees with the weakening of the principle of causality, one undermines at the same time the aforesaid doctrine. And, in the second place, though one may not say that the doctrine of Karma is so characteristic of modern Theosophy that it can never be dropped, in practice it is so important that one can hardly imagine the movement without it. In our opinion a Theosophist should, therefore, look for reasons to maintain and save the law of causality. Dr. Vreede, however, quotes with apparent approval the present-day opinions of physicists, and neglects the opponents of the far-reaching conclusions they draw from the present stage of their research.

What has just been said is more or less connected with the *Third Point*: The "subject-object method" would be wrong. Physicists have arrived at the conviction that observation changes the object. If one tackles a certain phenomenon in a certain way, waves seem to be involved; if it is tackled the other way round, particles. This is called "complementarity".[15] Now it is quite possible that many phenomena display two sides, and there is nothing against calling that complementarity. But we would prefer to be cautious with regard to complementarity in the strict, alternating sense as it seems to occur in nuclear physics. Things might turn out to be quite different. In our opinion the occultist has reasons to expect this and he might at least suspend his judgement. Mr. Leadbeater somewhere[16] writes about a certain tiny organ, with which hidden and subtle things can be observed. This is exactly what nuclear physics needs: very sensitive observation. In that case the influence of the subject or the observer on the object may very well be largely eliminated.[17]

What would be the general truth of Dr. Vreede's statement in Point 3: that the subject-object method should also be rejected outside physics and that Theosophists stressed *the* "*I*" too much?

Dr. Vreede here looks back in the history of thought. The anthropocentric starting point was initiated by René Descartes, and propagated by Auguste Comte and led to an extreme subjectivism ("the I as subject and all the rest as object") making sterile the whole of Occidental idealistic philosophy as well as the Oriental philosophies with their yoga practices: all of them are typically subjective. The *Theosophist*, accordingly, meditated too much on his own "*I*".[18]

Now, in our opinion, things probably came to pass in a slightly different way in the history of thought. First, one should not confound *the* "*I*" with "consciousness". It is true that Descartes spoke about "cogito", but the I was in that case not in the foreground (Fichte the elder was the first expressly to philosophize on the I), and by "cogito" he meant rather consciousness or mind. Of Descartes the strong opposition, the drastic dualism which he supposed to exist between mind or consciousness on the one side, and the body and matter in space on the other was very characteristic.[19] This Cartesian dualism had great consequences. Descartes himself was already inclined to consign the animals entirely to the body side. Later materialists [20] continued in this way; Lamettrie extended this idea to Man in his *L'homme machine* (1748). On the opposite side there were philosophers expounding that we, as a matter of fact, only know our consciousness directly, the existence of the outer world always being an inference *(Satz der Immanenz)*. This consideration constitutes the only tenable refutation of materialism. All the latter considerations were actually formulated by IMMANUEL KANT (1724-1804). It is in the context of Kantianism that the problem of subjectivism arises. According to a certain interpretation of his doctrine the things-in-themselves are not knowable. This is unsatisfactory, but one should point out that this merely subjective knowledge by his followers, the idealistic philosophers, was not meant as being subject to the personal errors of Mr. A. and Miss B. No, let the things-in-themselves be unknowable, in their appearances order reigns; the conception of the world arrived at in this way is not arbitrary. That is why we entirely disagree with the opinion akin to Dr. Vreede's voiced by the late Professor J. E. van der Stok (1958 †) on this problem of subjectivism and of epistemological idealism. All the idealistic philosophies of the West, and also those of the East, are (according to him) exceedingly subjective, they run in a vicious circle, they start and terminate with the self and do not emerge from their subjectivity. All this leads to disillusionment, and even to a cataclysm, for those philosophies are built upon the delusion of the self; they are nothing but vaingloriousness. The outer world, however, is man's better half; in the objective world, outside us, lies the real mystery.[21] This presentation of the matter is not only open to objection, but definitely wrong. We admit at once that unknowledgeability of things-in-themselves and of the outer world is far from satisfactory. Kantians who adhere to this have not found a true solution. This standpoint certainly is in want of completion.[22] However, it is not correct that *all* idealistic philosophies have got stuck in the vicious circle of the "I". For one thing, subjectivity in this case is, as we remarked, definitely not that of Mr. A or Miss B: the aim, here, also is to eleminate the personal error. All these, or nearly all these philosophers strive after a conception of the world having objective validity. It is about the very foundation of this objective validity (the *quaestio juris* of epistemology) that the battle rages among philosophers. If the establishment of such a foundation succeeds, the outer world can be known. We have endeavoured to make a contribution towards the solution of this problem in our *Tweeërlei Subjectiviteit.*[23] The basic thought therein is that difficulties arise, because a sufficiently sharp distinction was not made between the individual self or subject (the "infrasubject") and the One, real Self or Subject (the "suprasubject" or God). The battle, after all, concerns the validity of laws "a priori", such as causality, which everyone considers as true beforehand, a priori, independent of experience. Now Kant taught that every individual subject assimilates *(verarbeitet)* the data of experience causally (and in other *a priori* ways too). How, then, can this subject know what lies behind that assimilation? Therefore many Kantians contend that things-in-themselves are not knowable. On the other hand, others (and also *Tweeërlei Subjectiviteit)* hold the view that the assimilation of the data of experience need not detract from the validity of the result of the assimilation, if only the following is assumed: the One Suprasubject or God created, on the one hand, the laws obtaining in the world (for instance causality), and, on the other hand, planted a knowledge of them, an apriori conviction of their validity in us, in the infrasubjects. In this case we, the infrasubjects, are able to know certain things about the foundations of the world via the suprasubject-detour (this suprasubject of which we all are parts). Not only the apriori laws, but also the possibility of knowledge in general ("how can the subject ever reach the object?") can be established in this way, as we participate in the Basis of the World, which embraces all. In the same way subjectivism can be overcome, though it may be true that we start by knowing only our own consciousness. In that way, not only the wish to reach reality is uttered, but also the way thereto is, in principle, pointed out. Idealism is no longer subjective idealism, as, indirectly, a realism is attained. Professor van der Stok altogether neglects this possibility, the way out offered by this standpoint. It can certainly not be maintained that all idealistic philosophies should have got stuck in a subjectivism of the kind he means. But a knowledge of contemporaneous philosophy is obviously not a strong point of many theosophists.

Professor van der Stok goes on to say in that passage: "There, in the objective world, lies the real mystery, it is not in us, it is outside us". But we thought that God within us was at least as important as God without. We even thought that somehow He could be approached more easily within us than without. We thought that the immanence of God in every creature ("we are gods") was a teaching typical of Theosophy. Does the rejection of it also belong to "the new attitude"? Dr. Besant, however, used to speak about the One Self and the many small selves, teaching that the small selves were basically the One Self. Properly speaking, this is a Vedāntic doctrine. And the doctrine of twofold subjectivity, of the One Suprasubject as opposed to the many infrasubjects, is also Vedānta, Vedānta in terms of Western notions for Occidental thought. Should this Vedāntic strain also disappear from modern Theosophy?

Dr. Vreede writes that theosophists have concentrated too much on their own "I", meditating too often on the latter, thinking that they were meditating on the Higher Self.[24] Meanwhile, "*my* karma", "*my* incarnations" etc. were dwelled upon.[25] *Well, then they did it in the wrong way.* It may even be questioned whether all that meditation is in the Western's line. Anyhow, *the intention* has never been to meditate upon the lower self, but on *the* Self, the One, the Highest.

Now, to what extent should that subject-object method be rejected? If one understands by that, that the individual subject (and here actually in the sense of personal error) should be eliminated in view of achieving complete concentration on the object, on things as they really present themselves, then that seems to us to be the only correct method both for science and for occultism. Dr. Vreede is right that Mr. Leadbeater's great results were due to this.[26] One should not try to get rid of this method, but, on the contrary, continue to apply it. (A man like Mr. Geoffrey Hodson, not mentioned by Dr. Vreede, always endeavoured to do so, and not without success). In science, too, it is questionable, when scientists should acquiesce in the circumstance that the observer's influence should always prevent the object (in this case within nuclear physics) from being known. No more should the occultist approve of this, but rather hope that in this case clairvoyant research using refined organs will indicate a way out.

The article goes on to say that the ancient method produces a static picture.[27] But *while knowing*, Man always has to cut reality up into small parts. The *functional* attitude, which Dr. Vreede advocates (his *Point 4*) is a different one, not that of knowing. This seems to us to be what Dr. Vreede overlooks: it may be true that the intuition *(Einfühlung)* which he recommends with regard to the trees and to nature in general,[28] and sympathy and self-sacrifice [29] are excellent and to be valued highly, but they concern *other* functions of consciousness than that of knowing. They have their own value and significance; but one should not suffer them to trespass on the realm of knowledge. In that case the whole affair becomes confused, and the other function, that of knowing, is handicapped. We are well aware that other problems have to be considered, such as the knowledgeability of the Absolute. The Absolute can obviously never be known entirely. Here the "fundamental paradox" comes to the fore.[30] It is perhaps better not to enter into this point here.

When Dr. Vreede seeks to counterbalance a certain sterility, one could also say a certain depression, in the life of the Theosophical Society today, his "new attitude" is no remedy to us. We shall have to reconcile ourselves to the fact that personalities such as dr. Besant and their unparalleled inspiration are no longer among us, and we shall have to make the best of it as long as this situation lasts. There can never be a surfeit of functions such as mystic experiencing, action as sacrifice, devotion and *élan*. But they should not obscure that which is being taught. One should continue to ponder on the ancient teachings and the ancient methods and not scrap them in a hurry, when the science of the moment points in a particular direction, for instance towards the weakening of the principle of causality. Instead of looking for all sorts of new roads, one might join people who, like the occultist and author Geoffrey Hodson, seem to tread with success the old roads with their clear concepts.

We will end by saying something about what we called *Point 1:* the neglect of the *feminine* side of manifestation. There may be some truth in that. But the danger also exists of exaggerating one's reaction to that neglect. Did Dr. Besant really show in "The Ancient Wisdom" an inveterate masculine attitude? We can hardly see any essentially masculine symbols in the passage quoted. Moreover, can one expect the same of a person who always championed the rights of women, as she did? It is true that, apart from "The Ancient Wisdom", one often encounters representations of God as a man. Ignoring foolish anthropomorphism (the old gentleman with a beard) one should try and see the deeper meaning of it: the symbol of the relation between Spirit and Matter, in which the Masculine principle stands for the Spirit. Of Spirit and Matter Spirit is always the deeper, more important principle. If the use of this image of the Masculine gives offence, it is better to omit it. For the rest the champions of the feminine aspect of Deity certainly do mean by that something like Primary Matter (Mulaprakriti).

This is always one degree lower than the Spirit. In this manner one might even start worshipping something which is not the Highest. Meanwhile one could also view it in such a way that the Masculine principle forms the beginning and the Feminine principle the end.

This shows how much caution is needed with regard to these analogies and corresponding principles. The Pythagoreans already had their list of opposed principles.[31] Romanticists went in for triads.[32] Hegel in his dialectic method (thesis-antithesis-synthesis) raised this to a more philosophical level; but Hegelians sometimes try to bring too much different things into this scheme. Theosophists also show the tendency to see reality as being divided up into triads[33] and into other schemes. In our opinion we should be prudent here and consider that reality is probably far more complicated. When Prof. van der Stok for instance in dealing with the Western Union tries to connect the countries of Western Europe with the seven rays,[34] we question it. What we miss here is a pronouncement telling us whether all this only has the purpose of offering a convenient aid to meditation, or whether such schemes are actually *true*, the reflections of real inner relations, so that they cannot be rendered in any different way. This is not clearly stated, and many people obviously think the latter (whether such reflections are evident to them or not): that such schemes are not merely an expedient, but are intended to be truth.

Our general conclusion is that, if a new presentation of Theosophy should be needed, on no account should the clarity and common sense of a Dr. Besant and a Mr. Leadbeater be dropped. Enthusiasm and zest for Theosophy and for the endeavour to turn it into action should be present, but the cause of Theosophy is not furthered by novelties which can hardly be called clear-cut, and which in any case cannot bear comparison to the "neo-theosophy" of Dr. Besant and Mr. Leadbeater.

NOTES

[1] See *Theosofia*, Jan. and Febr. 1956, p. 6 *seq.* and *De betekenis en de taak der Theosofische Vereniging*, Amsterdam 1961, p. 63 *seq.*

[2] *The Theosophist*, June 1954, p. 173 *seq.* See also *Theosofia*, Oct. 1954, p. 145 *seq.* We shall quote this article as "A".

[3] *The Theosophist*, July 1955, p. 230 *seq.*; *Theosofia*, Oct. 1955, p. 173 *seq.* We quote this article as "B". A third paper which appeared in *The Theosophist* of Sept. 1955, p. 366 *seq.* did not call for comment.

[4] A p. 173.

[5] In many countries political parties, for instance, often change their names and yet pursue about the same ends.

[6] Roman Catholicism has discovered, rather late in the day, a social vocation, but so far hardly any with regard to animals. It has partly conformed to scientific theories about the age of the earth and the origin of species.

[7] A p. 177.

[8] B p. 235-236.

[9] B p. 239.

[10] A p. 175; B p. 236.

[11] A p. 179; B p. 237.

[12] Cp. L. de Broglie, *La physique quantitique restera-t-elle indéterministe?*, Paris 1953.

[13] Cp. our *Indeterminisme of Determinisme?*, Assen 1949, p. 8 *seq.* and in *De Grondparadox*, p. 184 *seq.*

[14] *Natuurwetenschap en Wijsbegeerte*, Utrecht 1946; *The Philosophy of Nature*, Pittsburgh 1953.

[15] B p. 240.

[16] See *The Inner Life*, II, p. 120; A. Besant, "Investigations into the Superphysical", *Adyar Pamphlet* nr. 36, p. 20.

[17] Cp. *Indeterminisme of Determinisme?*, p. 29, n. 15.

[18] B p. 231 *seq.*; A p. 175.

[19] Cp. *e.g.* our *Ochêma* I, p. 64 *seq.*

[20] Dr. Vreede writes that at the end of the 19th Century science, psychology and philosophy were all at a deadlock, suffocated in materialism (B p. 231). There is undoubtedly a certain amount of truth in that statement. However, several counterforces were already at work. F. A. Lange who in 1866 published his *Geschichte des Materialismus*, was no materialist but a Kantian (Cp. *Ochêma* I, p. 17 *seq.*). In addition to Neo-Kantianism Neo-Hegelianism sprang up (Professor Bolland in Holland). Psychic Monism of the Dutch philosopher Heymans and kindred philosophies elsewhere represented trends opposed to materialism. The thought at the back of the mind of many theosophical writers dealing with materialism of the second half of the 19th Century is: "and then Mme. Blavatsky's Theosophy came, and everything changed". The reversal, however, was, at least in the visible life of thought, certainly not due only to Theosophy. Conversely, in contemporaneous science enough materialism (now called physicalism which, for instance, disapproves of parapsychology) has remained.

[21] *St. Michael's News*, Dec. 1952 (XVI, 3), p. 28.

[22] Cp., for instance, our paper: "Moet het Kantianisme worden verlaten of voltooid?" (Should Kantianism be forsaken or completed?), *Mens en Kosmos* IX, p. 73 *seq.* and in *De Grondparadox*, p. 79 *seq.*

[23] Haarlem 1929. See *The Adyar Theosophist*, March 1930, p. 570. The problems concerned were summarized in *Drei Vorträge* . . . (Leiden 1939), p. 9 *seq.* and in the paper mentioned under 22).

[24] A p. 175.

[25] B p. 232.

[26] B p. 236.

[27] B p. 236.

[28] B p. 233.

[29] B p. 237.

[30] See above Ch. VII.

[31] Cp. C. J. de Vogel, *Greek Philosophy* I, (Leiden 1950), p. 19.
[32] Cp. R. Huch, *Ausbreitung und Verfall der Romantik*, p. 82 *seq.*
[33] Cp. our "Driedeeling", *Theosophia*, July 1921, p. 148 *seq.*
[34] *St. Michael's News*, July 1955, p. 147 *seq.*

INDEX

A SHORT BIOGRAPHY OF THE AUTHOR

Born at Rotterdam in 1896.

Member of the Theosophical Society (Adyar) since 1915.

Studied philosophy and psychology under Professor G. Heymans at Groningen University. Took a degree there corresponding to a M.A. in 1919.

Subsequently followed classes at the Universities of Hamburg, Geneva, Paris (Sorbonne) and Vienna.

Member of the Board of the Netherlands Society for Psychical Research, 1932-38.

Research Fellow in Philosophy in Harvard College, Cambridge, Mass., 1935-36.

Co-editor *Theosophia*, Organ of the Netherlands Section, Theosophical Society, 1935-41.

Head of the Sectional Library of the Netherlands Section, Theosophical Society, 1938-59.

Co-editor *Winkler Prins Encyclopedia* 1944-50.

External Lecturer in Metaphysics in Leyden University, 1945-53.

Ph.D. degree at Amsterdam University 1954.

Member of the Board of the Netherlands Theosophical Research Centre, 1954-today.

Professor of Metaphysics in the Spirit of Theosophy on behalf of the Foundation "Proclus" in Leyden University, 1958-today.

SOME WRITINGS BY THE AUTHOR

Tweeërlei Subjectiviteit (Twofold Subjectivity), Haarlem 1929.

Drei Vorträge über Philosophie und Parapsychologie (Three Lectures on Philosophy and Parapsychology), Leiden 1939.

Variaties op één en meer Themata (Variations on One and More Themes. Collected Essays), Leiden 1947.

Repertorium der Nederlandse Wijsbegeerte (Repertory of Dutch Philosophy), Amsterdam 1948; Supplement 1958.

De Theodicee, het Continuïteitsbeginsel en de Grondparadox (Theodicy, Principle of Continuity and Fundamental Paradox), Leiden 1951.

Ochêma, Geschiedenis en Zin van het Hylisch Pluralisme (Ochema, History and Import of Hylic Pluralism), Assen 1954.

Ochêma II, Het Hylisch Pluralisme in het Oosterse Denken (Hylic Pluralism in Eastern Thought), Assen 1958.

De Grondparadox en andere Voordrachten en Essays (The Fundamental Paradox and Other Addresses and Essays), Assen 1961.